9
'6

SOCIALIST HISTC

SOCIALIST HISTORY
OCCASIONAL PAPERS SERIES
No 25

THE NARODNIKS
IN THE
RUSSIAN REVOLUTION

RUSSIA'S SOCIALIST-
REVOLUTIONARIES IN 1917

FRANCIS KING
(translator and compiler)

2007

Dedicated to the memory of Monty Johnstone, 1928 – 2007,
who always took socialist ideas seriously,
even those he disagreed with.

Published by the Socialist History Society, 2007

ISBN 978-0-9555138-2-4

Typeset by SHS, 2007

www.socialisthistorysociety.co.uk

Contents

I. Foreword

Ninety years ago, in March 1917, Tsarism, in the shape of the Romanov dynasty which had ruled the Russian Empire for over 300 years, collapsed. For the first time, political parties were able to operate openly in Russia. They could publish papers, leaflets and pamphlets, they could recruit and organise, stand in elections, present their programmes, compete with one another. Throughout the empire, but especially in Russia proper, the political right virtually evaporated overnight, leaving the field to liberals and various hues of socialists. The party which enjoyed the greatest support throughout 1917 was the Socialist-Revolutionary Party, which took its inspiration from the old narodnik ("populist") revolutionaries of the 1860s and 1870s. Its policy of equitable land redistribution to those who worked it earned the party the loyalty of much of Russia's peasantry – an unusual achievement in Europe for an avowedly socialist organisation. However, the SR party proved unable to consolidate its popular sympathy into effective political power; it failed to prevent the Bolsheviks from taking power in November 1917 and their rapid destruction of the SR party as a significant political rival.

For all the time the heirs to the Bolsheviks, the Communist Party of the Soviet Union, remained in power, the defeat and eclipse of the other socialist traditions could be presented as something natural, as the necessary outcome of a struggle between the Bolsheviks' correct ideas and their rivals' incorrect ones. This was the view invariably put forward in Soviet historiography right up to 1991. Socialist and left-wing historians outside the USSR also largely ignored the SRs and their ideas – those writers who disliked Bolshevism were generally more inclined to look to the Mensheviks or the anarchists. There are, however, some good reasons why the SRs and some of their ideas – particularly their agrarian policies – may deserve more serious attention on the left. Peasant radicalism remains a potent force in various parts of the world today, not least in Latin America, whilst in developed countries many on the left are now trying to combine socialism with green critiques of industrial society. In some respects, the narodniks and their successors, the SRs, can be regarded as pioneers of both peasant-based and non-industrial socialism. On the other hand, the story of the SRs in 1917 represents a cautionary tale for left-wing forces everywhere – the SRs started that year with overwhelming support among both workers and peasants, and squandered much of it pursuing policies and programmes that were not their own.

As far as mainstream historiography is concerned, for some years the only major works in English were Oliver Radkey's two excellent studies: *The Agrarian Foes of Bolshevism* (1958) and *Sickle under the Hammer* (1963). In 1976, Maureen Perrie published a study of the SRs' agrarian policy in 1905-07, but it is only more recently the party has begun to receive greater attention, notably in the work of Michael Melancon, who has produced several first-rate studies on the SRs.

The change in the Russian-language literature, however, has been much more marked. In Soviet times, especially after the early 1930s, when the publication of documentary histories more or less ceased, the few Russian-language books on the party were tendentious accounts of its "bankruptcy" and "collapse". Since 1991, there has been a steady stream of high-quality historical studies and monographs on the parties, movements and personalities of 1917. The greatest single contribution has been made by ROSSPEN, the publishers of the Russian Political Encyclopaedia. In addition to numerous monographs, since 1996 ROSSPEN has been publishing an excellent series of documentary histories under the general heading "Political Parties of Russia at the end of the 19th and in the first third of the 20th centuries". Many of the documents translated in this pamphlet are taken from these volumes.

In compiling this publication, my aim has been to mark the 90th anniversary of 1917 by presenting SR perspectives that year to an English-speaking readership, thereby providing a narrative of events from interesting and unfamiliar standpoints. I am not arguing that the SRs represented some kind of missed chance for Russia. Accidents in history are rare: there are sound reasons why it was the Bolsheviks, not the SRs, who prevailed in 1917, just as there are sound reasons why the Bolsheviks' successor, the CPSU, lost power again in 1991. Nor am I urging that Aleksandr Kerensky, Viktor Chernov, Mariya Spiridonova or any other SR leaders should replace Vladimir Lenin as a revolutionary icon. Iconography has nothing to do with serious history. The SRs, like all the other socialist organisations and tendencies which existed or exist around the world, are part of the heritage of socialism. They all have their insights and their illusions, achievements and failures, merits and deficiencies, and all are worthy of sympathetic, but critical, study.

Several people have assisted me in preparing this publication by providing materials or making editorial suggestions. I would like to thank Richard Deswarte, David Morgan and Willie Thompson for their comments on my drafts, John Biggart and Matthias Neumann for bringing books over from Russia, and Sally Davison of Lawrence & Wishart publishers for permission to reproduce document 20. Naturally, I take full responsibility for any textual, factual or ideological errors that may have slipped through.

Calendars, transliteration and other editorial questions
Russia did not adopt the Gregorian calendar used in the rest of Europe until 1 (14) February 1918. In 1917, Russian dates were 13 days behind Western dates. The period covered in the pamphlet predates the calendar reform, and so all dates within that period are given in their contemporary Russian form. Thus May Day was celebrated on 18 April 1917 according to the Russian calendar, etc.

In transliterating from Russian into English I have broadly followed the traditional British transliteration system, but with certain surnames given in their most familiar forms (e.g. Trotsky, Zinoviev). The least familiar Russian words have been italicised.

The sources for the documents reproduced follow each document. I have inserted a few brief explanatory remarks in the documents themselves using square brackets. A few longer explanations, and sources for direct quotations in the commentaries, are given in footnotes. Otherwise, I have tried to keep footnotes to a bare minimum. Where there is no ellipsis [...], the document has been translated in its entirety, as given in the source indicated. Any other parentheses, emphases etc. in the documents are in accordance with the original.

Several other documents of Russian and Soviet history that I have translated for various purposes in the past can be accessed on my academic translations website www.korolevperevody.co.uk/korolev. I can also be contacted via that site.

Francis King, November 2007

Document 1. Programme of the Socialist-Revolutionary Party (abridged)

The State System

1. The establishment of a democratic republic with broad autonomy for regions and communities; the greatest possible application of the federative principle in relation to individual nationalities, the recognition of their unconditional right to self-determination; a direct, secret, equal and universal right to vote for any citizen aged 20 or over, without distinction of sex, religion or nationality; proportional representation; direct popular legislation (through referenda and initiatives); all officials to be elected, recallable at any time and subject to the law; complete freedom of conscience, speech, the press, assembly, for workers' strikes and unions; complete and general civil equality; inviolability of the person and home; the complete separation of church and state and religion to be a private matter for everyone; the establishment of compulsory, general, secular education for all at state expense; equality of languages; access to the courts free of charge; the abolition of the standing army and its replacement by a people's militia.

The Labour Question

1. The speediest possible reduction in the working day (in the short term – to 8 hours in most branches of industry, and correspondingly less in dangerous or unhealthy branches); the establishment of minimum wages by agreement between the local authorities and the workers' unions; comprehensive state insurance paid for by the state and employers and administered by the insured workers themselves; legal protection for labour in all branches of industry and trade, in accordance with the requirements of health and safety and supervised by a factory inspectorate elected by the workers; (normal working conditions, sanitary workplaces, a ban on employing under-16s, restrictions on employing minors, prohibition of women's and children's work in certain branches of production and at certain times, sufficient unbroken time off every week etc.); trade union organisation for workers with an increasing role in determining the internal organisation of industrial enterprises.

Agrarian and economic questions

1. The socialisation of all privately-owned lands, i.e. they should cease to be the private property of individual persons and become social property, administered by democratically organised unions of village communes, on the basis of equal land use.

2. The introduction of a progressive tax on income and inheritance, with complete freedom from taxation of all small incomes below a certain norm; the abolition of indirect taxes (except on luxury items), protective tariffs and all taxes on labour.

3. The development of all kinds of social services – free medical care, the organisation of agronomy services, the communalisation of water supply, street lighting and communications; urban and rural communities to have the widest powers to tax and compulsorily acquire landed property; communal zemstvo* and state policies favouring the development of cooperation on strictly democratic principles.

4. The workers are to be warned away from that "state socialism" which is partly a system of half measures to lull the working class and partly a peculiar form of state capitalism.

5. The immediate revolutionary struggle against the autocracy and the convocation of a Zemskiy Sobor (a Constituent Assembly), freely elected by all citizens without distinction of sex, caste, nationality or religion to liquidate the autocratic regime and reconstruct the entire existing order.

The Socialist-Revolutionary Party will both put forward this programme in the Constituent Assembly and strive to implement it directly in the revolutionary period.

Source: *Sbornik Programm Russkikh Politicheskikh Partiy*, Skitalets, Petrograd, 1917, pp. 11 – 13.

---

*Zemstvos were rural local authorities, established in much of European Russia after 1864. They were elected on an unequal franchise, which gave disproportionate weight to the nobility. They were in charge of local economic management – public services, education, health and sanitary services – but were expressly forbidden from playing any "political" role. In 1917 they were re-elected on an equal franchise. The equivalent body for urban areas was called a "duma".

II. Background

Narodniks and Marxists

"Narodism" (from "*narod*" - "the people"; sometimes translated as "populism") was a revolutionary current which emerged in Russia after the abolition of peasant serfdom in 1861. The revolutionary narodniks of the 1870s and 1880s, the organisation *Narodnaya volya* ("People's Will"), were the common ancestor of both the Marxists (the Russian Social-Democratic Workers' Party) and the SRs. Narodnik ideology postulated that a form of socialism could be built in Russia, based directly on the collectivist traditions and forms of common land ownership of the Russian countryside. In this way, Russia could avoid the traumas of capitalist development experienced in Western Europe.

In the early 1880s, a group of narodniks around Georgiy Plekhanov rejected that view. Instead, they adopted a version of Marxism, arguing that capitalism was already breaking down the Russian village communes, and that Russia's path to socialism lay through the further development of capitalism and the emergence of a proletariat. The peasantry, they believed, was destined to break down into a small class of rural landowning capitalists, and a much larger class of landless rural proletarians. Although Marx himself, a few years beforehand, had been prepared to accept the possibility that Russia could avoid the "fatal vicissitudes of the capitalist regime",* Russian Marxism, as elaborated by Plekhanov and his colleagues, regarded Russia as backward rather than special. The country, they contended, was fated to follow the path of development pioneered by capitalism in Western Europe. The Russian Marxists also differentiated themselves from the narodniks on questions of tactics - for example, they rejected the use of political assassination ("terror") in the struggle against the autocracy as inexpedient. Indeed, *Narodnaya volya*'s greatest success in this regard, the assassination of the (relatively) liberal Tsar Alexander II in 1881, had simply resulted in 13 years of rule by his far more reactionary son, Alexander III.

By the 1890s, many of the old narodnik nostrums had become untenable. Capitalism, industry and trade were developing fast in Russia, and Marxism was gaining popularity among the intelligentsia as an ideology better able to explain these new phenomena. Those who embraced Marxism included many former narodniks. However, that did not necessarily mean that the Marxists had won the argument. A lively debate continued between Marxist and narodnik intellectuals about how far capitalism was breaking down the old collectivist relationships in the countryside, and whether the village commune and the widespread Russian peasant objection to the "ownership" of land would be able to resist capitalist encroachments. Moreover, there were unmistakable signs that the Russian peasantry had some potential as a revolutionary class. Peasants resented the ongoing redemption payments payable to the former serf-owning landlords following emancipation, and coveted the large portions of land still held by that class. A peasant movement for land reform was

---

* See Karl Marx's letter of November 1877 to the editorial board of *Otechestvennye zapiski*, in Karl Marx and Frederick Engels, *Selected Correspondence*, Progress, Moscow, 1975, p. 292

developing around the turn of the century with demands that chimed with those of narodism.

In response, in the late 1890s the scattered circles of narodniks that remained in Russia began to regroup around a revised ideology that took account of the changes in Russia since the 1870s. A key figure in this rethinking, and thereafter the major ideologist of the SR party throughout its history, was Viktor Chernov. Chernov, who had been a revolutionary since his schooldays, had been exiled to Tambov in the latter half of the 1890s, where he organised workers' circles and Russia's first revolutionary peasant brotherhood. In 1899 he met the veteran narodnik N K Mikhailovsky, who urged him to "Europeanise" narodism and develop a socialist ideology suitable for overwhelmingly agrarian societies like Russia. When the Socialist-Revolutionary Party was formed from various narodnik circles in 1901-02, Chernov became the editor of its newspaper, *Revolyutsionnaya Rossiya*.

The new SR ideology was not hostile to Marx – he was duly honoured as one of the great socialist thinkers of the previous century. The language and thinking of the SRs were permeated with Marxian concepts. They were proud to be part of the Second International (they affiliated in 1904), and regarded Marxist parties abroad as their comrades. But they entirely rejected the view that capitalist relations were destined to penetrate the Russian countryside, and that the peasantry, as a class of small proprietors, were "petty bourgeois", as some Marxists would have it. The SRs played down the class differences between peasants and industrial workers, presenting them all as one "*trudovoy narod*" (working people), ranged against a common enemy, the "exploiters". The fact that many Russian industrial workers retained their ties with the villages was not seen as a sign of "backwardness", but as further proof of this affinity between the toiling classes. SRs reproached the Russian Marxists – not without foundation – for turning Marx's observations on the historical experience of Western Europe into some kind of universal law of development, applicable everywhere. Marxist ideologists, for their part, often dismissed the SRs as a "bourgeois" or "petty-bourgeois" organisation, which sought to represent a class, the peasantry, which was destined to fragment into rural exploiters (rich peasants) and rural poor (landless labourers).

On the ground, however, these ideological differences often had little significance. Individuals, and sometimes entire local groups, could change their orientation between social-democracy (Marxism) and SRism; there were many free-floating socialists in Russia who worked with whatever people happened to be around locally. Moreover, right up to 1917, SRs and Marxists worked together underground against a common enemy – the autocracy and its police. In this regard, far more united them than divided them.

The first Russian revolution and afterwards
The SRs followed their forebears in *Narodnaya volya* in regarding political assassination as a useful method of struggle. Their preferred targets were particularly reactionary state and police officials. Their first high-profile act, a few months after the party's foundation, was to kill the Interior Minister D S Sipyagin in 1902, followed by his

successor, V K Pleve, in 1904. A special "fighting organisation" of the party was formed specifically for this work. It was headed from 1903 to 1908 by Evno Azef, a key figure in the party in the early years, and possibly the most notorious double agent in the history of revolutionary politics. But while "terrorism" was the most striking aspect of the party's activities, it was very much subsidiary to its main concerns of spreading its influence through propaganda and agitation. On the eve of the 1905 revolution, the SRs had between two and three thousand members in Russia, and although they directed their appeal to peasants and workers, the bulk of these members were students, intellectuals or white-collar workers.

In the revolutionary ferment of the years 1905-07, the SRs, like the social-democrats, experienced very rapid growth. Membership reached 50–60,000, mainly workers and peasants; it dominated the Peasant Union and was strong in some other trade unions. The SR conception of revolution had certain differences from those of the Marxists. Marxist schemas, with certain variations, envisaged a "bourgeois-democratic" revolution that would overthrow Tsarism and the pre-capitalist remnants of Russia's social and political structure, and introduce political freedoms. The institution of private property would remain largely untouched. After a period of bourgeois rule and capitalist development, the working class and its organisations would become strong enough to overthrow capitalism and the capitalists in a second, socialist revolution. In contrast, the SR schema envisaged a single revolution to overthrow Tsarism, end the caste privileges of the nobility, and also abolish private property in land, with all the land being declared the property of the people, to be granted on an equitable basis to those who worked it. A constituent assembly would be convened, and Russia would become a democratic parliamentary republic. Once political freedoms had been won, most SRs envisaged Russia's subsequent transition to socialism as a gradual, evolutionary process.

The ebbing of the revolutionary tide after 1906 and the subsequent reaction and state repression hit the SRs hard. The prospect of equitable land reform, a democratic constitution and political freedom seemed as far off as ever. Many party leaders had to return into exile abroad, others were arrested or went underground. The SRs had never been a well-organised party, and they declined more precipitately than the social-democrats, who were better organised and more firmly ensconced in the trade unions. On their far left, a Union of Socialist-Revolutionary Maximalists formed. This group criticised the main SR party for half-heartedness, demanded nothing less than the maximum socialist programme, and rapidly burnt itself out in an intense campaign of "terrorism". On the right, a group of writers and intellectuals around the respected narodnik journal *Russkoe bogatstvo* urged that the party abandon all underground and armed activity and seek to operate legally within the narrow bounds permitted by the Tsarist state after October 1905. When the first SR congress in 1906 refused to approve this step, this group broke away to form the People's Socialist Party (NS, in its Russian acronym). A much more serious crisis for the party erupted in 1908, when it was revealed that Evno Azef, head of the SR fighting organisation and a key figure in the party itself, had been working for the Tsarist secret police for the past 15 years. This scandal largely discredited "terrorism" as a tactic within the party. The old leadership, including Chernov, resigned in 1909, and a new leadership, untainted by association with Azef, was chosen – only to be arrested shortly thereafter.

The SRs' internal crisis was exacerbated by the agrarian reforms sponsored by the Prime Minister, P A Stolypin, who sought to ensure that Russia had no more peasant uprisings by turning peasants into petty proprietors on the Western model. Thus, peasant households acquired the right to leave the village communes and consolidate their share of the village land into a compact holding which became their private property. Stolpyin hoped that this measure, which he termed a "wager on the strong", would help modernise Russian agriculture, erode the institution of the village commune, and turn the most energetic peasants into supporters of the existing order. Stolypin's reform threatened to undermine the entire collectivist basis of the Russian agrarian socialism. This, combined with the brutal measures Stolypin employed to pacify the countryside after 1906, made him a particular hate figure, and in 1911 he was assassinated by Dmitriy Bogrov, a former SR Maximalist.

During this "period of reaction" SR political work amongst peasants was at a very low ebb. Such SR organisations that survived at all were mainly among urban workers, while many individual SRs in the countryside devoted their efforts to the growing peasant co-operative sector. However, in the last few years before the war, the fortunes of the Russian labour movement and Russian socialism began to revive, and this also benefited the Socialist-Revolutionaries. In urban and industrial areas, they worked alongside social-democrats (Bolsheviks and Mensheviks), anarcho-syndicalists and others in trade unions and other workers' organisations, student bodies and suchlike. To co-ordinate this activity, members of all the socialist organisations in a given area often formed joint committees. On these day-to-day questions the positions of the different parties were, more often than not, indistinguishable.

World War 1

The SRs had enthusiastically supported the Second International's celebrated resolutions against war in 1907, 1910 and 1912. But when the war actually came in the summer of 1914, the SRs, like the social-democrats, divided into pro- and anti-war camps. Anti-war ("internationalist") sentiment was much stronger among Russian socialists than most other European socialists because Russia was in no serious danger of being overrun, and socialists had no stake whatsoever in the existing Tsarist order. Nonetheless, the division cut right through the SR party, just as it split the Menshevik faction of social-democracy. The arguments and considerations were identical in both parties. Among the SR émigré leadership, pro-war ("defencist") figures like N D Avksent'ev, V V Rudnev and the veteran narodnik Ekaterina Breshko-Breshkovskaya, argued that German militarism was the greater enemy, that Russia was allied with the democracies of Europe, and that democratic reform would have to wait until after victory, at which point it would become inevitable. The anti-war group, led by Chernov and another veteran narodnik, Mark Natanson, argued that the war was a conflict between two rival imperialist blocs, that no good would come from a Russian victory, and that there should be no let up in political and economic agitation.

Chernov and Natanson participated in the Zimmerwald and Kienthal conferences of internationalist socialists in 1915 and 1916. Within Russia the same divisions existed, although the SRs who remained active in the underground, by dint of their situation, tended increasingly towards the internationalist, anti-war line.

However, Russia's poor showing in the war and the evident incompetence of the Tsarist administration meant that even defencist-patriotic SRs could not trust the government to prosecute the war successfully. In 1915, a secret conference of People's Socialists, SRs and Trudoviks (narodnik-inclined Duma deputies and their supporters), convened by the Duma deputy Aleksandr Kerensky, resolved to launch a "struggle for a decisive change in the system of state administration".* This was part of a much wider wave of disillusionment and discontent with the government on the part of "respectable" society, which by early 1917 had eroded almost all the support for Nicholas II in Russia. For the SRs, however, the need to get rid of the Tsar was almost the last issue on which the party spoke with one voice.

Aleksandr Fedorovich Kerensky

---

* Cited in G Anoprieva, N Erofeev, "Partiya sotsialistov-revolyutsionerov", in V V Shelokhaev et al., eds, *Politicheskie partii Rossii. Konets XIX - pervaya tret' XX veka*, ROSSPEN, Moscow, 1996, p. 440.

III. The February Revolution

While liberal and moderate socialist politicians were plotting regime change in the hope of pursuing the war more effectively and saving Russia from catastrophe, socialist and labour movement activists in the industrial and working-class areas of Russia's big cities were also busy organising. Food shortages, rising prices, poor working conditions and myriad other grievances had led to waves of strikes and protest actions throughout 1916. Intense secret police activity to arrest revolutionaries and socialists in the cities had failed to quell the growing workers' movement. To coordinate their actions, the different socialist groups operating in these areas again formed blocs, joint committees and networks. Similar developments were taking place in the garrisons and at the front, where many arrested revolutionaries had been sent as a punishment. In the last few months before Tsarism fell, SRs, Bolsheviks, Mensheviks, independent social-democrats and others collaborated more actively than before against their common enemy. Resources – not least printing presses – were pooled as the socialist activists attempted to channel, direct and extend the strikes and protests into a powerful movement against the government. In the capital, Petrograd, two informal blocs emerged: a left bloc of radical SRs, the Petersburg RSDRP inter-district committee (*mezhrayonka*), Bolsheviks and internationalist Mensheviks; and a right bloc of moderate SRs and defencist Mensheviks.

The following appeal to soldiers in Petrograd was issued by the Petrograd SRs and the social-democratic *mezhrayonka* – very much part of the left bloc – on 27 February 1917. By this stage there had already been four days of strikes and mass demonstrations on the streets of Petrograd, and some of the Cossacks and soldiers sent to quell the demonstrations had refused to obey orders. On that same day the right socialists took the initiative in founding the Petrograd Soviet, while liberal Duma deputies from the Constitutional-Democratic (Kadet) party joined with left deputies and others to form a Provisional Duma Committee, in defiance of a government order dissolving the Duma. The government was losing control.

Document 2. Appeal of the Petersburg* inter-district committee of the RS-DRP and the PSR

27 February 1917

In struggle you will find your rights!
Workers of the world unite!

Comrade Soldiers!

The working class, driven by hunger, has risen in struggle with your and our enemies, in struggle against the war, and against the autocracy of our criminal

---

* At the outbreak of war with Germany, the official (German-sounding) name of St Petersburg had been Russified to Petrograd. Certain anti-war political groups in the city pointedly retained the old nomenclature.

rulers. It has risen in struggle for freedom and land! Comrades! For 2½ years you have been suffering in trenches and barracks, for 2½ years you have been tormented by your inhuman commanding officers. The soldier's lot is a hard one. You are treated no better than dogs. Comrades! Brothers! Your hopes lie with us! We place our hopes in you! We extend our calloused hands, crippled with work, to you. Brothers! Some of you have shot at the people. Workers' blood has been shed! Soldiers! Do not stain your hands with the blood of your brothers! Down with fratricide! Glory and honour to those of you who supported the people! Honour to the Cossacks who drove the city police out of the Znamenie cathedral! Honour to the soldiers of the Pavlovsky regiment who avenged the violence of the city police! Brothers! If you are ordered to shoot at the people, shoot those who gave you the orders. Let your bayonets be turned against the oppressors. Our starving wives await your help. Comrades! Read our leaflets! Organise yourselves! Join up with the workers! It is our sacred belief that the soldiers will not betray the people! Brothers! Hear our voice! Long live the unity of the army and the people! Down with the autocracy! Down with the war! Long live the revolution! All the land to the peasants! Full freedom to the people!

Petersburg inter-district committee of the RS-DRP
Party of Socialist-Revolutionaries.

Archive source: GARF 1741/1/35278
Published in O A Shashkova, compiler, *Fevral'skaya revolyutsiya 1917: sbornik dokumentov i materialov,* Rossiyskiy gosudarstvennyy gumanitarnyy universitet, Moscow, 1996, p.79.

News of events in Petrograd travelled fast, and by the next day a similar appeal – including denunciations of the war – was issued by the Moscow SRs.

Document 3. Leaflet of the Moscow Organisation Group of the PSR

28 February 1917

In struggle you will find your rights!

From the 24th right up to the 27th of February, crowds of starving people, thousands strong, have been out on the streets of Petrograd, demanding bread. The people have risen in revolt, and the government has been using machine-gun and rifle fire to disperse them. When the State Duma, under pressure from the mass movement, demanded that the government hand over the organisation of food supplies to public organisations, the government dissolved the Duma by royal decree. The Preobrazhensky, Volynsky, Semenovsky, Pavlovsky and other guards regiments have come over to the side of the people's rising, and the State Duma is continuing its activities under their protection. The Arsenal has been seized by the people and the soldiers. The Vyborg and Peter-Paul prisons have released their inmates.

These were yesterday's events.

Comrades! The whole country must rise with the Petrograd workers and soldiers. The decisive hour has struck. A determined and unwavering assault is needed. Everyone, to the last man, must stop work. Elect your representatives without delay to the Soviet of Workers' Deputies, which must take on the role of government in Moscow together with other organisations. There is power in a concerted assault.

Long live the people in arms! Long live the national Constituent Assembly! Down with the autocracy! Down with the war! Long live the revolution!

Moscow Organisation Group of the Socialist-Revolutionary Party

Archive source: OPI RIM f. 424, d. 163, l. 2

Published in O A Shashkova, compiler, *Fevral'skaya revolyutsiya 1917: sbornik dokumentov i materialov,* Rossiyskiy gosudarstvennyy gumanitarnyy universitet, Moscow, 1996, p. 242.

Events moved swiftly. On 28 February the Petrograd Soviet published the first issue of its *Izvestiya,* which helped stimulate the formation of soviets across Russia, and on 1 March it called on soldiers to elect their own committees. The next day, 2 March, General M V Alekseev persuaded Tsar Nicholas II to abdicate, and the Provisional Duma Committee created a Provisional Government to take over the reins of power. The mainly right socialist leadership of the Petrograd Soviet promised to support this new government "insofar as" it acted in line with the general aims of the Soviet.

A key figure in both the Petrograd Soviet and the Duma Committee at this stage was Aleksandr Kerensky, a right-wing SR, lawyer and freemason. Although the Soviet had resolved – for both ideological and practical reasons – not to involve itself directly in government, the liberal politicians in the Duma committee were very keen to have one or two moderate socialists in the government. Kerensky was offered the post of Justice Minister, which he accepted. The following speech, in which he sold this *fait accompli* to the Soviet with great aplomb, was typical of his oratorical style.

Document 4. *Izvestiya* report of Kerensky's speech to the Petrograd Soviet

2 March 1917

Comrades, do you trust me? (Calls from all benches: "We trust you! We trust you!") I say to you, comrades, from the depths of my heart, that I am ready to die, if need be. (Commotion in the hall. A F Kerensky acknowledges the extended applause, which turns into a lengthy ovation.) Comrades, given that a new government was being organised, I had to give an immediate reply, without waiting for your formal sanction, to the offer that I should take the post of Minister of Justice. (Stormy applause, general enthusiasm.) Comrades, I had the representatives of the old government in my hands, and I could not agree to let them go. (Stormy applause, cries of "Quite right!") I accepted the offer and joined the new Provisional Government as Justice Minister. (General applause and cries of "Bravo!") My first act was to order the immediate release of all political prisoners without exception, and to bring back from Siberia with full honours our comrades, the social-democratic Duma deputies. (Loud applause, general enthusiasm.) Given that I took on the position of Justice Minister before getting your formal authorisation, I am resigning my position as a vice chair of the Soviet of workers' deputies. But I am prepared to resume this role if you think it necessary. (Stormy applause and general calls: "Please do, please do!") Comrades, in joining the Provisional Government, I remain what I have always been, I remain a republican. (Noisy applause.) I declared to the Provisional Government that I am a representative of the democracy,* and that the Provisional Government should regard me as expressing the demands of the democracy. It should pay particular attention to the views that I will be defending as a representative of that democracy whose efforts overthrew the old regime. Comrades, we have no time to lose, every minute is precious. I call on you to be organised, to be disciplined, and to support us, your representatives, who are ready to die for the people and who have devoted their lives to the people.

Source: *Izvestiya* No. 4, 3 March 1917, p. 2
Published in B D Gal'perina, compiler, *Petrogradskiy Sovet Rabochikh i Soldatskikh Deputatov*, Vol. 1, Nauka, Leningrad, 1991, pp. 77 – 78.

It would be hard to overstate the extent to which the fortunes of the SR party had changed in the course of just one week. From being a small, persecuted group, operating largely underground in the cities with almost no organisation in the countryside, it was thrust into the centre of the political stage. It had become one of the parties of government, and for the first few months after February, Kerensky's popularity across Russia was immense. The party had a massive influx of members – workers, peasants, soldiers, intellectuals. At last it was able to direct its attention to the countryside again, where it found a receptive audience among Russia's peasants. But as the party came out into the open and grew, so too, over the subsequent months, did the tensions and divisions within that party.

One immediate result of this change of fortune was an ascendancy of the right-wing and moderate SRs in the party. There were several reasons for this, mainly stemming from the view that the revolution was still very fragile; it had to be consolidated. The mood in the vast Russian hinterland was uncertain. The army top

---

* In addition to its more usual meaning of "rule by the people", "democracy" (*demokratiya*) was widely used in 1917 to denote "the working people and their organisations", as distinct from the "census" (propertied) social strata. In translation, this second meaning has often been rendered into English as "the democracy".

brass had played a central part in deposing the Tsar, in the hope that it would help Russia's war effort, and a radical anti-war programme could push them back towards restoration. For the moderate and right SRs, the overriding concern was to sustain the alliance of anti-Tsarist forces until a Constituent Assembly could be convened to draw up a democratic constitution. And in the first few weeks of the revolution, everyone, left and right, could share in the general elation at the fall of the Tsar.

Scene from the February revolution

IV. What to do about the war?

Before February, enthusiasm within the SR party for Russia's war effort had been restricted to the party's right wing. Although the opposite position of defeatism was held by an even smaller minority, much of the party was broadly anti-war, equating the war effort with fighting for the autocracy. After February, this position changed radically. Germany's ruling circles, quite correctly, saw the Russian revolution not as an opportunity to achieve a just peace, but as a chance to weaken and subdue their enemy on the Eastern front. Russian socialists, on the other hand, now had a motherland, they had their freedoms, the gains of the revolution, to defend. The hard core of right-wing defencists were now joined by a much larger group of "revolutionary defencists", anxious to secure Russia's new liberty against German imperialism until such time as a just peace could be secured. A resolution of the Moscow SR conference, which began on 3 March, illustrated this thinking:

Document 5. Resolution of the First Moscow Conference of SRs "On the War"

mid-March 1917

This Moscow conference is not concerned with the question of who bears the immediate responsibility for starting the war, the roots of which, in the final analysis, lie in the basic contradictions of the capitalist system. Since international democracy proved powerless, for various reasons, to prevent the conflict, the conference recognises the right to self-defence of the democracy of each nation. In the present situation, this right to self-defence means that Russian democracy has both the right and the duty to defend the people's freedom won by the revolution. The conference expresses its support for the appeal of the Petrograd Soviet of Workers' and Soldiers' Deputies. It considers that in order to end the war as quickly as possible and in view of the urgent need to restore the International, Russian democracy should not abandon or disorganise the defence of the country, but should, on the contrary, support it as far as possible. At the same time it must wage a relentless struggle against the annexationist aims of the ruling classes. In particular, it must demand that the Provisional Government specifically declares that it renounces any territorial seizures or any reparations. It must demand that the Government be prepared to embark on peace talks immediately, in agreement with the democracies of the Allied countries. These should be based on a recognition of the right of every people to self-determination. Furthermore, the Russian democracy must make an urgent appeal to the working classes of all nations, both allied and hostile, to struggle against all policies of territorial seizure; to wage a revolutionary struggle to democratise their systems. This would be the best means of ensuring that peace is concluded as soon as possible.

Source: *Delo naroda* No. 9, 25 March 1917
Published in N D Erofeev, compiler, *Partiya sotsialistov-revolyutsionerov. Dokumenty i materialy*, Vol 3, part 1. ROSSPEN, Moscow, 2000, p. 31.

In the first few weeks of the revolution, when everything still seemed possible, such formulations could satisfy most members of the party, defencists as well as internationalists. But it soon became apparent that the working classes of all nations were not about to compel their governments to conclude a just peace, and, specifically, that the working classes of Germany were not about to stop their government and armies pressing home their advantage against a weakened Russia. Just a few weeks later, at the Second Petrograd SR Conference on 3 April, the party showed itself to be thoroughly divided on what to do about the war. One speaker even made the normally taboo suggestion of a separate peace with Germany. The main report, arguing the "revolutionary defencist" case for continuing the war effort, was given by the veteran SR leader Abram Gots. Before the February revolution, Gots had been a leading figure among the "Siberian Zimmerwaldists" – a group of SRs and Mensheviks in Siberian exile who supported the position of the Zimmerwald conference of internationalist socialists in 1915. In this report, Gots eloquently presented the policy of the SR right wing in the language of the party's left wing.

Document 6. A R Gots: "The war and the Socialist-Revolutionary Party". Report to the Petrograd SR conference (slightly abridged).

3 April 1917

Comrades, I have been given the responsible task of reporting to you on the main, central question of the present day. The question of war and peace in the present situation is the question of questions. The fate of the revolution, of all its political and social gains, and of the revolutionary movement itself depends on us finding the correct solution to this question. The country is anxious to hear from the leading revolutionary socialist parties of the day. It urgently needs clear and firm decisions from them, because the time for interminable discussions, academic debates and concoctions has passed. ... The answer that you give, the position you take on the war, as representatives of the SR party's Petrograd organisation, is important. For this very reason I appeal to you not to content yourselves with adopting elastic resolutions with multiple meanings, but to give a precise, vivid answer, excluding any possibility of twisted or ambiguous interpretation. It is better for a political party to give a wrong, but vivid response, than to flounder about helplessly with vague formulae and so on.

But, comrades, in this respect the task you have before you today has been made significantly easier by such authoritative and influential bodies as the Petrograd Soviet of Workers' and Soldiers' Deputies and the All-Russia meeting of delegates of workers' and soldiers' soviets. The question of the war was posed at the All-Russia meeting, and the voice of the revolutionary people – the proletariat, and the rebellious army – has already spoken, vividly, inspiringly, and eloquently. And we, representatives of the SR party, who claim to express the wishes and aspirations of the revolutionary and socialist democracy, should certainly take account of this imposing, highly significant expression of democracy's will. ...

We regard the present war as an imperialist war, brought about by clashes of interests within aggressive international capital. A struggle for world hegemony, for domination of world markets underlies the present unprecedentedly bloody conflict between nations. A lust for power, an uncontrollable drive to extend the sphere of capitalist domination, a quite spontaneous urge to seize the markets of backward countries – these are the mainsprings of international finance capital. The whole capitalist world has divided into coalitions of powers, which are equally animated by the same urge to world domination. We are not in the least inclined to idealise the imperialist policies of any of the participants in this global slaughter. On the contrary, it is vital that we declare categorically to the whole world: the imperialist circles of all the belligerent states are responsible for this war. Not one of the bourgeois classes of the countries engulfed by war is free of this responsibility. The bourgeois classes and the social-chauvinist press that serves their interests may try to whitewash their own governments and shift all the blame onto their opponents, but that is just a political manoeuvre, aimed at blunting the socialist consciousness of the working masses. We reject, just as firmly, any attempt to regard the present imperialist war as a war of liberation, as a war for right and justice, to defend the rights of enslaved nationalities. For the capitalist systems of all countries, this war is equally aggressive. Likewise, for the working classes of all nations it is something that has been forced upon them by the ruling classes. They have dragged their peoples into this slaughter for interests which are not the peoples' interests.

...The war was brought about by the clash of interests of international capital. It can and must be ended by the efforts of international democracy, ended on an *international* basis. This presents the democracy of all countries with two fundamental, inextricably linked, tasks. The first task is an unrelenting, unceasing struggle against the annexationist, imperialist intentions of the ruling classes of our own countries. The second is to re-create the International, the main bastion of international peace, which the war has destroyed. Democracy should be devoting its efforts to this, and those socialist elements who have remained true to the banner of international socialism are already working to this end. At first they were weak, atomised, without wide support. But as the war has gone on, these elements have become stronger, developed, acquired influence among the working masses, even though they cannot yet impose their will on the ruling classes.

Of all the politically enserfed peoples, only the Russian democracy, relying on all the living forces within the country, has managed to overthrow that old power that hung over Russia like a terrible nightmare. In three days the rebellious army and the Petrograd working class smashed the rotten edifice of Tsarism. They unleashed the social and political creativity of a great people. A country that had remained silent for years, imprisoned by dark forces, stifled in the embrace of reaction, was reborn in one great surge of revolutionary enthusiasm. It sprouted, at fantastic speed, a network of revolutionary-democratic organisations, the Soviets of Workers' and Soldiers' Deputies. And the democracy has become master of the revolutionary situation, in practice if not formally. It is the dominant, leading force in the country. Not one important step in domestic or foreign policy may now be taken without its consent. Russian democracy is now the force which bears responsibility for the fate of the country. It is now faced with immense tasks of social and political construction. This obliges us to reconsider our *tactical* attitude to the war, rather than our attitude in principle. Tactics, comrades, as the saying goes, can change in 24 hours, especially if in those 24 hours a great revolution has taken place, the like of which the world has never seen. The great Russian revolution, which has placed the democracy at the head of the nation, must fundamentally change our tactical attitude to the war.

We should say directly: the Russian revolutionary democracy has fulfilled honourably, and continues to fulfil, its internationalist obligations as the vanguard of the international socialist movement. The first words that the victorious Russian democracy addressed to the peoples of the belligerent countries was a call for peace without annexations, indemnities or seizures, for peace on the basis of national self-determination. Russian democracy solemnly declared to the world, that it had broken decisively with the foreign policy of Tsarism, and was not going to allow a great people to become the blind instrument of the imperialist policies either of the Russian, or of the Anglo-French bourgeoisie. But it did not limit itself to this manifesto alone. Russian democracy immediately launched a systematic campaign against the imperialist policies of our bourgeoisie. It put pressure on the Provisional Government and urged it to declare officially that it had broken with the policy of territorial seizures and renounced all annexationist intentions. As we know, this campaign was successful. The Provisional Government's declaration, made under pressure from the revolutionary democracy, solemnly declared that it had broken with the old Tsarist foreign policy. This declaration by the Provisional Government must be regarded as one of the most important gains of the Russian revolution on the way to democratising foreign policy, as one of the greatest achievements of international democracy. ... We can already see clearly the next pressing tasks for socialist democracy to resolve. First and foremost, we shall have to exert additional pressure on our Provisional Government to take the initiative in summoning a conference of the Allies to work out a peace programme eschewing annexations, territorial seizures and reparations. Then we shall have to convene an international conference of socialists from *all* the belligerent countries in order to resurrect the International and work out common international measures to bring about the speediest end to the war.

What our revolutionary democracy has done so far is quite enough for us to say that we have fulfilled our international obligations as the vanguard of the international socialist movement honourably. But our democracy is not only the vanguard of the international movement. It is also the leader of our own national revolutionary movement. And fulfilling its obligations as the leader of the all-national revolutionary movement is just as sacred as fulfilling its obligations to the International. This is made easier by the fact that these two tasks are essentially one, because, in defending our new-born freedom from external encroachments, physically shielding the social and political gains of our revolution from attack, guarding our liberated motherland, we are thereby assisting the cause of the International. After all, Russian democracy is now the mainstay of the international socialist movement, its main fortress and bastion. The Russian revolution has been the first openly to compel its government to go down the road of renouncing annexation. If the revolution were to be routed, that would be an irreparable calamity for the whole International. If the Russian revolution were to fall now under the blows of German militarism, that would not only be the end of our freedom, but a death sentence on those internationalist currents in Germany who are close to us in spirit. And this obliges all the socialist parties in Russia, and the SR party in particular, to answer this basic question openly and directly: do we accept our obligation to defend our revolution and country not only against counterrevolutionary attempts from within, but also against enemy encroachments from without? And we are profoundly convinced that the SR party can only give one answer: yes, we do. And in the present circumstances, when Russian democracy has fulfilled and is continuing to fulfil its obligations to the International, it can do so with a clear conscience. ...

We are also told that all the time Russia remains part of a coalition pursuing imperialist plans overall, it shares responsibility for the policy of the coalition. Therefore – we are told – there can be no question of re-examining the problem of defence. These notions are based on a primitive vulgarisation of the principles of internationalist socialism. People who think like this forget that our main task is not to liberate Russian capital from the clutches of Anglo-French capital because, as soon as it had been freed from the influence of Allied capital, it would collapse into the embrace of German capital. It could not be any other way, if we bear in mind the complex, entwined and criss-crossed network of relationships entangling the whole sphere of international capitalist relations. This capital, with its international interconnections, can only be opposed by the method of international action, by co-ordinating the efforts of the democracies of all countries. Therefore we decisively reject the path of separate agreements, which fundamentally reject the method of international agreement and action.

... Say firmly, that the socialist democracy will fulfil its international duty completely, but it will fulfil its duty to its liberated motherland no less decisively. Say clearly that now, when the democracy bears responsibility for the fate of the revolution and the country, it will devote all its efforts to defend the freedom it has won against every encroachment of German imperialism, to organise the defence of the gains of the revolution.

Say loudly that to undermine the front is to undermine the revolution.

Source: *Delo naroda*, No. 16, 5 April 1917.
Published in N D Erofeev, compiler, *Partiya sotisialistov-revolyutsionerov. Dokumenty i materialy*, Vol. 3 part 1, ROSSPEN, Moscow, 2000, pp. 51 – 56.

The discussion that ensued covered almost the full range of positions on the war within the SR party. Gots's main opponent was Boris Kamkov, who later became one of the leaders of the Left SR party and, for a brief period in 1918, a member of Lenin's government.

Document 7. Account in *Delo naroda* of the discussion on Gots's report on the war

3 April 1917

Immediately after this **B Kamkov** presented a wide-ranging counter-report, in which he described the reporter's position as "social-patriotic with international trimmings".

Kamkov declared, "the causes of the war are imperialist on both sides. And at the present time we, the Russian democracy, are also members of a coalition of villains. Although we have renounced annexations and reparations, the Anglo-French bourgeoisie has not. We must clearly and definitively guard against formulations like those of the French and German social-chauvinists, to the effect that we are defending ourselves against German imperialism. The Russian revolution changes nothing as far as our internationalist position on the war is concerned.

"We categorically reject the social-patriotic notion of 'defencism', which destroyed the great citadel of the Second International. 'Defence of the Russian revolution' would oblige us to accept all that chauvinism, the German 'Burgfrieden', the French 'Union sacrée'. Our actions should be directed towards liquidating the war, but Russian democracy has done almost nothing in this direction, or, rather, it has done the bare minimum, not the maximum that should have been done.

"In its declaration, the bourgeois Provisional Government recognised all the treaties and contracts which the Tsarist government had concluded with Britain and France behind the backs of the people. And as long as our allies have not renounced their programme of conquest, even greedier than that of Austria-Germany, then we are waging a war of plunder in the interests, at least, of the Anglo-French bourgeoisie. This point needs to be made clearly and firmly."

The speaker then set out some basic tactical steps in three directions: 1) the convocation of an international socialist congress; 2) pressure on the Provisional Government to oblige it to publish the earlier international treaties concluded by Russia, and 3) pressure on the Provisional Government to work out a plan for peace and call on the Allies to attend a peace conference.

Kamkov concluded, "Our task is not to hide behind 'defensive' formulae, but to carry the revolutionary movement into all countries and bring about that 'worldwide conflagration' in which the present bourgeois society will be burned up and a socialist society will be created!"

Speaking for the 2nd Baltic crew members and the Kronstadt sailors, **Klement'ev** declared forcefully that slogans like "down with the war!" will create a counterrevolutionary movement among the sailors.

Pumpyansky, the next speaker, declared passionately that "dreams are one thing, but reality is another. On our days off we can dream our beautiful dreams, but from day to day we have to live in reality, with its genuine blood and real suffering. Not one of the 'defencists' is denying that all war is imperialist. But we are not fighting for the non-existent annexationist aims of England and France, nor will the Russian revolution allow them to try that sort of 'petty blackmail'. The Russian revolution has changed the course of the war, it has declared for peace, and that is an enormous achievement. But until the workers' democracy of Germany takes our outstretched hand, there will be no 'conflagration'. We should not proclaim 'throw down your weapons!', but 'prepare to fight to defend freedom'."

Following a short speech by **Bol'shakov**, who declared that "not one of the socialist-internationalists wants defeat", **Lebedev** spoke, pointing out that slogans for an immediate end to the war would not only fail to attract the sympathy of England and France, but would dangerously isolate Russia.

Batrak stressed that a new element had been brought into the imperialist war, the element of a struggle for freedom, a revolutionary war. "So long as there is a danger that Wilhelm might restore Nicholas, so long as world democracy has not finalised its attitude to the war, we should not be calling for 'an immediate end to the war'. We should reject the formula of 'peace at any price' and stand for the defence of the gains of the revolution."

V Trutovsky spoke energetically: "Do not forget the pledges that we made at the Basel and Stuttgart socialist congresses. At that time we socialists promised the International to struggle with all our might to put an end to the war, if one should break out. So once a war breaks out, we must struggle to put an end to it. We should throw off the yoke of the governments of England and France, and should not be afraid of being isolated. Russia's allies are the backward capitalist countries, the countries to the east of us, not those to the west.

"We should conclude a separate peace with Germany if it renounces reparations and annexations, and the working class will be with us in that!"

"I am happy for the Russian people," declared **P Sorokin** fervently, "who have shown greater political sense and historical understanding than our internationalist comrades. Those who call for breaking the treaties with England and France would not only lead Russia into isolation, but to the possibility of war with our current allies. A separate peace is neither one thing nor the other, a desire to 'keep your innocence and make a bit of money'. Those who are calling for this should not forget that they are taking on the responsibility for the 160 million-strong Russian people, and that the revolution is a matter of life and death for them! You should not risk human lives with your fine words and magnificent phrases!" The speaker then discussed Kamkov and the internationalists' resolution in detail.

Il'insky said, "Defence should be understood in the way it is understood by the Soviet of Workers' and Soldiers' Deputies. We should only call off our offensive when the Red Flag is flying over Potsdamer Platz. It was not theory that shattered the International, it was just a dream anyway. We cannot allow bare, abstract theses to remain 'just as they were', these inactivated theses, because they will lead to disorganisation. Our army's crusade, the renaissance of Russian freedom, must not be interrupted, so long as we can see Hindenburg rather than Liebknecht on the opposite side of our winding trenches.

Petrovsky-Il'enko: "We are faced with the fact of war, and we cannot walk away from it while German bayonets are ranged against us. Russia's happiness lies in its renewal, and a victory over German imperialism will be a victory for European democracy."

"All the disagreements between the 'internationalists' and the 'defencists'," said **A Gizetti**, "lie in the internationalists' belief that the social revolution may be close at hand. But all the time we cannot be sure of that, the army and the people need clear and definite slogans."

Gus'kov: "We are responsible to the International. The speaker's [Gots's] resolution is unacceptable, because it remains quiet about what we ought to do if our allies do not renounce their annexationist policies. We should not be sanctifying war, but marching at the head of the people under the banner of socialism."

In **Kovarsky**'s view, it is vital to retain the "defencist" outlook until the German coalition sets out its peace conditions clearly.

A Gukovsky rejected reconciling the different views on the war, because the "internationalist" current in party thinking was close to the Marxists, while the "defencist" was the genuine social-revolutionary, people's-will position.

Chikhachev pointed out that a separate peace would bring Russia to a new war and destroy the International at the same time.

Utgof declared that although the army wants peace, it cannot just stand and do nothing, "remain organised just where it is", because that would be suicidal and ruinous. ...

Holding to his point of view, **Kamkov** stressed that "the task of the party is not to support the front but to work creatively to rebuild the International".

A Gots, the main speaker, elaborating the standpoint developed in his report and motion, declared that the party was not abandoning the task of recreating the International, but nor could it refuse to defend social and political gains against attack from without.

With this reply by the main speaker, the resolution was sent to the compositing commission and the first day of the conference came to a close.

Source: *Delo naroda*, No. 17, 6 April 1917.
Published in N D Erofeev, compiler, *Partiya sotisialistov-revolyutsionerov. Dokumenty i materialy*, Vol. 3 part 1, ROSSPEN, Moscow, 2000, pp. 37 – 40.

Abram Rafailovich Gots

V. The "April Crisis": the SRs join the government

Abram Gots's conviction that the Provisional Government had signed up to the Soviet's foreign policy proved misplaced when it emerged that Foreign Minister Pavel Milyukov, a leading member of the liberal Kadet party, had written to his counterparts in the Allied countries assuring them that Russia's war aims remained unchanged. This was taken to mean that the government, for all its assurances to the Soviet, still aimed at annexing Constantinople and turning the Black Sea, in effect, into a Russian lake. The ensuing scandal, towards the end of April 1917, provoked the first major crisis in the Provisional Government. There were anti-war demonstrations on the streets of Petrograd, and the Soviet leaders, their strategy in tatters, had to reconsider their attitude to power. In the Petrograd Soviet Executive Committee, Viktor Chernov, newly returned from exile abroad, agonised over the situation.

Document 8. From the stenographer's note of Chernov's speech at the Petrograd Soviet EC

19 April 1917

...We see the strength of the organised army of labour growing, not just from day to day but from hour to hour. The difference there was at first between Petrograd and the provinces is disappearing with each passing day. The development of the peasantry represents additional forces ... up to now, we thought that it would be imprudent for us to form a government. Our position is strengthening every day. Maybe it will not be up to us when all the power comes to us. We are quite relaxed about this. We are well aware that we are struggling for power, but not forcing the issue.

...Where did the Provisional Government find the strength to mount this challenge? Which has deeper roots in the popular masses – the democratic organisations or the Provisional Government? We could always overthrow it, but has the time for that come yet? Evidently, the Provisional Government is relying on some force or other...

...Our revolutionary patriotism dictates that we cannot let Milyukov's challenge pass unanswered. The revolution has so much momentum that it cannot be stopped. ... All our forces could unite around the slogan "Down with Milyukov". We need to combine the Russian revolution with an Anglo-French one... We [the Soviet] created our own secret diplomacy in the form of the Contact Commission [for liaison with the government]. But it was not us exerting pressure on the government, but the other way around. ... Now the situation is different. Now we could take power into our own hands, and the people would be with us. However, should we do this?

Source: TsGA SPb (formerly TsGAOR Leningrad) f. 1000, op. 73, d. 25. Published in *Voprosy istorii*, No. 4, 1990, pp. 11 – 12.

Chernov did not toy with the idea of overthrowing the Provisional Government for long. At sessions of the Soviet EC and the full Soviet the next day, Mark Broydo, for the Mensheviks, declared that to do so would be a "fatal mistake". The Trudovik Vladimir Stankevich suggested that some of the portfolios be taken by Soviet representatives. The Provisional Government had much the same idea – the Prime Minister, Prince Georgiy L'vov, urged the Soviet to share power in a coalition government in order to overcome the crisis. This was made easier by the departure of two of the least popular right-wing ministers: War Minister Aleksandr Guchkov and Foreign Minister Milyukov. For the Menshevik leaders in the Soviet, this still meant abandoning one of their hallowed dogmas – that in a "bourgeois-democratic" revolution, Marxists should be in opposition, not in government. For their SR allies, there was no question of principle at stake – Kerensky had been a minister from the outset. The debate among the SRs concerned the expediency of sharing the responsibility for the deeds and misdeeds of a government in which socialists would still be a minority.

A plenary session of the Petrograd Soviet on 1 May had approved the idea of Soviet representatives serving in the government. On 3 May, a conference of SR organisations in and around Petrograd considered the question. The right-wing SR Nikolay Avksent'ev opened proceedings:

Document 9. From N D Avksent'ev's speech to the conference of Petrograd SR organisations

3 May 1917

...Everything that has been happening gives the impression that the Russian state is collapsing. And if the democracy has become the master in this state, it should take on the task of governing it. And the Executive Committee considered itself bound to take a step forward and take part in the Provisional Government. Many of the far left socialists regard this as a betrayal of socialism. They claim that we will have the same sort of collaboration between socialists and the bourgeoisie as they have had in Western Europe, which has merely compromised the socialists.

No, comrades, we will not have that sort of collaboration here, because we are in the middle of a revolution, because the revolution is developing, the revolution is growing and broadening out. In our case governmental power is being levelled out in a leftward direction, as a series of government measures and personnel changes within that government attest. There is therefore no analogy between the introduction of one or two socialists into Western European governments and what is happening here.

It is on this basis that the Soviet EC, and subsequently the full Soviet resolved that if we are to get over this domestic and foreign crisis, there is only one way – by joining the revolutionary Provisional Government.

You are aware of the appeal that Prime Minister Prince L'vov made to the chairman of the Soviet of Workers' and Soldiers' Deputies Chkheidze. Invited to give its opinion on how a new government could be formed, the EC worked out a definite programme, on the basis of which socialists could join the government. The programme boils down to the following points. In foreign policy – accelerating the struggle for peace, insofar as that can be a matter for governments. That is – to convene a conference as quickly as possible to consider the latest international situation and work out the basis for a democratic peace. On the other hand, the army must be decisively democratised, to make it fit to fight to defend revolutionary Russia until the moment comes when international democracy can impose its will. All administrative institutions must be democratised. In the agrarian sphere – a series of measures to prepare for transferring the land to those who work it, and in labour policy – the broadest platform.

The EC has one final condition for entering the government: Minister Milyukov must not remain Foreign Minister.

That, in general outline, is the programme proposed by the Executive Committee...

Source: *Delo naroda*, No. 41, 5 May 1917.
Published in N D Erofeev, compiler, *Partiya sotisialistov-revolyutsionerov. Dokumenty i materialy*, Vol. 3 part 1, ROSSPEN, Moscow, 2000, pp. 97 – 98.

Boris Kamkov, for the SR left, had other ideas, as *Delo naroda* reported:

Document 10. Kamkov's contribution to the discussion

3 May 1917

Comrade **Kamkov** spoke against SRs joining a coalition Provisional Government. In comrade Kamkov's view, the crisis was not a question of the composition of the Provisional Government, but of its entire policy. Until the Provisional Government sets about ending the war and a complete democratic reorganisation of the country, any Provisional Government will just be hanging in the air. Any coalition government, of whatever composition, would be unable to break with the imperialist Allied powers. Only a government put forward by the soviets of workers', peasants' and soldiers' deputies would be able to break with the imperialists, renounce conquest and reorganise the country on democratic lines. The only way out is to form such a government, everything else is just a compromise that will not get us out of this blind alley and ruin.

Source: *Delo naroda*, No. 40, 4 May 1917.
Published in N D Erofeev, compiler, *Partiya sotisialistov-revolyutsionerov. Dokumenty i materialy*, Vol. 3 part 1, ROSSPEN, Moscow, 2000, p. 94.

But Kamkov was in a minority. Chernov, who took the portfolio of Agriculture Minister once his party had approved the coalition, asked rhetorically whether his party felt ready to assume the full responsibility of power in an all-socialist government, to take on and defeat the propertied classes and counterrevolution. If so, then of course it was duty bound to do so...

Document 11. From V M Chernov's speech to the conference of Petrograd SR organisations

3 May 1917

...But if not, and we cannot leap from the first month of pregnancy to the ninth, then we have to find some middle way. This middle way is a temporary sharing of power between propertied Russia and toiling Russia.

What can we gain from this? A great deal. We gain from the fact that with the resignation of Milyukov, with that great moral and political victory for workers' democracy, the Foreign Ministry will at last become a transmission mechanism for expressing the new orientation of toiling Russia on matters of war and peace. It will reinforce that orientation on the world scene. It is hard to overstate the inflammatory effect of those constant chauvinist statements from that doctrinaire advocate of an inflated, artificial, Russian quasi-imperialism. An end to all that is a gain in itself, and positive steps in the opposite direction will be better still. We are convinced that Russia's initiative can give impetus to workers' democracy in the Allied countries. Even the most intractable governments, under pressure from this democracy, will have in the end to renounce their grasping aims in this war. These steps will help ensure an end to the war and bring the beginning of peace negotiations closer. Because to rid the Allied camp of any remnants of annexationist policies would make things easier for the democracy in those Central powers with which we are at war. It would destroy the "holy alliance" of left and right and lead to internal disturbances. However these ended, they would be another "plus" from the point of view of a successful struggle for democratic peace terms. The entry of socialists into the government will strengthen and reinforce Russia's role ... as a base for a "third force", making its voice heard amidst this clash of international imperialists. Two approaches to achieving this suggest themselves. On one side, the workers' democracy can work to convene a conference of the workers of all countries to work out the conditions for a lasting democratic peace, and on the other side, the government can exert pressure on the Allied countries to take steps in the same direction, and of course, the second approach will be nurtured and helped along by the first. There is another condition. If we want to bring about the sort of national enthusiasm in the country that would ensure that the national will were taken into account, then we must ensure the correct domestic policies. This means that in two areas - labour and agriculture - socialists must hold positions. The Ministry of Labour, for example, should be given to the social-democrats. This is not because we have given them a monopoly over the urban proletariat or consider them better able to represent it - I think that we could already give them a run for their money if it came to a contest for dominance among the workers - but because we need to preserve the unity of the movement, make concessions for that unity and avoid unnecessary quarrels. On labour questions our day-to-day policies are sufficiently like those of the social-democrats to ensure that our cause would not suffer by that portfolio being granted to the social-democrats. On the land question, we need to ensure that there is a broad policy pursued, aimed unambiguously at transferring the land to those who work it. We envisage that transfer will take the form of socialisation of the land. This idea was initially supported only by a few people, then by a smallish group, and then by a party. Even recently most people considered it to be a utopia. We want to make it a reality. But in order to do so, we must prepare the relevant draft legislation for the Constituent Assembly. We must gather together all the information, all the factual and statistical data. It is also necessary that the policies governing the actual use of land *prior to* the Constituent Assembly do not lead us *away* from this solution to the agrarian question - which enjoys the support of almost everyone in Russia who works on the land - but towards this solution. It is also vital that socialists are in charge of the questions of food and supply, as these can only be solved correctly if we are committed to bold experiments, requisitions, nationalisations and municipalisations wherever necessary. And finally, it is essential that the revolutionary army and navy are not in the hands of people from the old world, but of representatives of the socialist vanguard of the movement. These battle posts - labour, food supply, agriculture, and the army - should be occupied by people from the workers', socialist, democracy...

Source: *Delo naroda*, No. 45, 10 May 1917.
Published in N D Erofeev, compiler, *Partiya sotisialistov-revolyutsionerov. Dokumenty i materialy*, Vol. 3 part 1, ROSSPEN, Moscow, 2000, pp. 104 - 106.

Chernov and Avksent'ev's resolution in favour of entering a coalition government won easily. Kerensky, who had joined the government on his own account as a member of the Duma, was now joined by five other socialists from the Petrograd Soviet. Chernov took over as Agriculture Minister, Kerensky became War Minister, the People's Socialist A V Peshekhonov became Food Minister. The other socialists in the first coalition were the Trudovik P N Pereverzev (Justice), and the Mensheviks I G Tsereteli (Posts and Telegraphs) and M I Skobelev (Labour). The political crisis was resolved - for the time being. But the increased public trust in the government went hand in hand with increased public expectations. Chernov, in his speech, had listed many of the good things that were supposed to flow from socialist participation in the government. The fortunes of the SR party, and particularly of its leadership, were now inextricably entwined with those of the Provisional Government. It had staked its credibility on rapid and radical progress on land reform, food supply, and the search for peace. It had promised more than it could possibly deliver.

VI. The Narodnik landscape after February

Before continuing the story into the summer of 1917, it is worth looking in a little more detail at the different groups advocating some form of narodnik socialism at that time. The situation in 1917 was very fluid, people moved from one group to another, some were active in more than one organisation. Sometimes groups merged, although more often they tended to split. In the first few months of the revolution, the significant all-Russia groups, beside the main SR party itself, were the Trudoviks and the People's Socialists (known by their Russian acronym as NSs) on the right, and the SR Maximalists on the far left. Additionally, there were several parties active among national minorities which adopted some version of narodnik socialism as a social programme to complement their nationalist programmes. These included the Armenian Dashnaktsutyun, which had existed since 1890 but only embraced socialism in 1907, the Socialist-Federalists in Georgia, the Ukrainian Party of Socialist-Revolutionaries, and the Belorussian Socialist Society (*Gramada*).

The SR party, larger than all these other parties taken together, contained several factions, including a strong internationalist left wing around Mariya Spiridonova, Mark Natanson, Kamkov and others, which finally split away in November 1917 to form the Party of Left Socialist Revolutionaries. Chernov and his colleagues represented the centre ground, while an articulate right wing around people like Boris Savinkov, the former "terrorist" leader, and the sociologist Pitirim Sorokin advocated political caution at home and strong support for the war effort. Naturally, each main faction had its own paper: by late spring the left controlled *Zemlya i volya* ("Land and Freedom"), officially the paper of the SR northern region; the official central party paper, which generally expressed Chernov's line, was *Delo naroda* ("The Cause of the People"); while *Volya naroda* ("People's Will") was the mouthpiece of the right.

Nonetheless, in the early months of the revolution in particular, there was a strong demand for unity, which neither party nor factional leaders could ignore. Indeed, they were all wholeheartedly in favour of unity – on their own terms. At the Petrograd SR conference in early April, Vladimir Zenzinov, a close aide of Kerensky, spoke eloquently *for* a unified socialist party in principle, and *against* doing anything about it in practice.

Document 12. From V M Zenzinov's report on the attitude of the Socialist-Revolutionary Party to other socialist and democratic organisations

3 April 1917

...Those of us who were active in the party and fervently believed in the force of the party's ideas during the worst years of the collapse of party life - in the period of intense government repression and the internal disorganisation resulting from the Azef affair – can now look to the future with profound moral satisfaction. The idea of the party as a whole has come back to life with renewed vigour. Many of the slogans our party proclaimed 15 years ago, which some greeted with amazement and others with protest, have now become the slogans of the Russian revolution. Our demand, "all the land to the whole people", which distinguished us so sharply from other parties in the past, is now accepted by all socialist and democratic parties, and has been heard and adopted by the mass of the people. We can state boldly that it will soon be put into effect.

This month of freedom has shown that the Socialist-Revolutionary Party, which not so long ago was being written off not only by our enemies, but also – sad to say – by some of our friends, is attracting wide sections of the population. For example, after just a few weeks' feverish work in the Petrograd organisations we have now registered about 5000 people in the various districts. Of the 400 delegates to the all-Russia meeting of workers' and soldiers' Soviets on 28 March, around 70 joined the Socialist-Revolutionary faction. At the all-Russia co-operative congress, which has just finished in Moscow, no fewer than 150 of the 400 co-operators present were our party comrades. We all know from our own observations that meetings called by the Socialist-Revolutionary Party get a good turnout. We can note all this with pride, because they show that our hard work in the past, with the irreplaceable losses our party suffered in its harsh struggle with the enemy, are now bearing fruit. Nevertheless, we should regard our successes and achievements coolly and cautiously. In the confusing and dangerous period of a revolutionary upsurge, all sorts of people rally to socialist and revolutionary parties. We too will get our share of people who have not fully or finally defined themselves politically. We should bear that in mind, if we wish to avoid cruel disappointments in the future.

We are currently going through the process of forming the party. We are all working to create an open Socialist-Revolutionary Party, but at the same time we must appreciate the need to define the precise contours of a party with its own distinctive features, which set it apart from the other socialist parties and delineate it sharply from the merely democratic groupings. During the period of illegality and harsh struggle with the authorities our party was able to express itself. In its programme it posed the question of the land and the peasantry firmly and clearly, and it has now lived to see the day where that most characteristic point in our programme has become the slogan of the entire movement. In the tactical sphere, the revolutionary initiative and selflessness shown by our party, which distinguished it from the other revolutionary parties, has found its justification in the armed overthrow [of Tsarism] which has just taken place. It is vital that this distinctive features of our party work, which have now been vindicated by life itself and which have distinguished our party from all the others, should continue to express themselves. In future as now, our party must remain a party of the whole working people, an active revolutionary party.

We should therefore develop firm but at the same time cautious tactics for building the party. Our position with regard to other socialist parties and democratic groupings should be clearly defined. We have never suffered from factionalism and intolerance. From our first appearance 17 years ago, we extended the hand of friendship to the other socialist parties. Our call at that time went unheeded. Today we reaffirm our fervent desire to see a united socialist party in Russia. We passionately want it, we know that it is essential, we believe that it is possible. But at the same time we are convinced that the time has not yet come. If we were to set to work on this immediately, it would mean that we had failed to assess the present position coolly enough. Before we call for our party to merge with the social-democratic party, we must first complete the establishment of the Socialist-Revolutionary Party. The question of merging with the social-democratic party should be posed in a practical way only when we exist as a unified party, as a real political party living a normal life, with all its organs, having devised a programme and tactics for the new conditions at a party-wide conference. One cannot change one's plans halfway through rebuilding one's house, when the foundations have already been laid. We can work more successfully for the unification of all socialist Russia if we undertake it as a party which is already established. This attitude does not, of course, preclude the possibility and necessity of joint practical work on current questions in the soviets of workers' and soldiers' deputies, in day to day municipal work, in the trade unions and the co-operative movement. Here we should work hand in hand with the social-democrats where there are no differences of principle between us in those areas, but at the same time we should retain and express our own party characteristics. On a broader scale we cannot fail to recognise the desirability of an all-socialist bloc of all the parties who view politics from the standpoint of the working classes.

Our relationship with the narodnik groups, the People's Socialists and the Trudoviks, is a special question. It has arisen everywhere, both in the centres and in the provinces. We should keep cool heads here as well. Undoubtedly, the new political situation has smoothed over many of the disagreements which divided us. There is a desire to unite and merge amongst the Socialist Revolutionaries, the People's Socialists and the Trudoviks alike. But is precisely the similarity between these three currents which should make us especially cautious in the way we deal with this question in practice. A hasty and unconditional merger with the People's Socialists would threaten to undermine the principles of international socialism which lie at the base of our programme. The entry of an amorphous mass of Trudoviks into our party could loosen up our ranks and make the socialist character of our party less distinct. And the basic tenets of international socialism and recognition of the class struggle should be unshakeable for us. And therefore for the sake of the Socialist-Revolutionary Party, which has already gone down in history as one of the revolutionary forces, in order that it should develop correctly in future, and, finally, in the interests of the eventual unification of the socialist parties into a united socialist party, we should not hurry to join with the People's Socialists and Trudoviks....

Our party has always been distinguished by its spirit of free criticism, but at the same time, happily, the spirit of intolerance and factionalism has always been alien to it. We have always dreamed of a united socialist party. And now we are convinced that the unification of both socialist parties is possible and necessary. But the unification will be more complete and correct once both parties have completed the process of party building which is still underway. We should therefore devote all our efforts towards creating and unifying our own party. Before the question of unification can be posed in practice, we should work in solidarity with other socialist parties in the sphere of practical politics, in so far as we have a common basis. But in the course of that work we should try to express our own party peculiarities which distinguish our party from the others.

As for unification with the narodnik groups, this question must be set aside as a practical matter until the process of forming our party has been completed. A firm and definite party line will also induce the narodnik groups to adopt more consistent principled positions and hasten the moment when the People's Socialists and the Trudoviks join our party.

Comrades, I call on you to work, by means of thorough organisation and firm and well-defined politics, for the unification of all socialist parties and groups into a single all-Russia socialist party.

Source: *Delo naroda*, No. 18, 7 April 1917.
Published in N D Erofeev, compiler, *Partiya sotisialistov-revolyutsionerov. Dokumenty i materialy*, Vol. 3 part 1, ROSSPEN, Moscow, 2000, pp. 71 - 75.

Although the SR leadership resisted any organisational unification with any other parties, in the Soviet executive they formed a very stable bloc with the main body of Mensheviks. While the SRs had a much larger base of support among the population, the Mensheviks largely determined the political line of this bloc. This was a peculiar state of affairs, given that the SRs did not share the Mensheviks' rather rigid Marxism, as the left SR Mariya Spiridonova pointed out:

Document 13. Mariya Spiridonova. From "The Tasks of the Revolution"

August 1917

...At any given moment in any individual country, socialist parties prioritise a certain part of their demands as the most pressing, the most essential for the immediate future. Along with the demands of the maximum part of the programme, and in the name of these demands, minimum demands arise. They are entirely determined by the historical situation of the struggle, and may be changed in all sorts of ways by considerations of practical expediency. But they have to be socialist through and through, and to be in complete accord with the principal part of the programme. The immediacy of the minimum part of the programme must never mean the distortion or even abandonment of revolutionary socialism.

The minimum programme refers to all those social and political demands intended for the period before the working class wins power, that is, for the period of the bourgeois revolution (agrarian reform, the 8-hour working day, a minimum wage, protection for labour, political freedom etc.) A particular feature of the Socialist-Revolutionary Party's minimum programme, and its main difference from the social-democratic one, is that SR demands in the sphere of social relations go way beyond the boundaries of the existing economic system. The social-democratic minimum programme only demands those improvements in the conditions of wage labour and the position of the working class that would not in themselves undermine the basis of bourgeois-democratic society.

The programmatic differences between social-democrats and socialist-revolutionaries around their minimum demands relate to very important differences in the two schools' ideas about the very conditions of social development. This is in its turn linked with more fundamental differences of view about the philosophical and economic preconditions which should underlie the scientific basis of socialism.

Maybe we socialist-revolutionaries could work with the social-democrats (Mensheviks) to build a socialist society in the future, but we cannot achieve it with them now. To unite with them now means to bend the whole content of our programme to fit the confines of the bourgeois order, an order which they are actively assisting, establishing and reinforcing. Their heads are hopelessly stuffed full of Marxist dogma, while their consciences permit a political opportunism (conciliationism) unprecedented in the history of the young socialist parties. These "socialists", in spite of the historic course of events, in spite of the whole socio-political conjuncture, are themselves blocking the path of a popular movement which is developing widely and has long surpassed the boundaries, stockades and fortifications of a bourgeois revolution.

To declare at the present time, in theory and in practice, that our revolution is bourgeois, to rely on those notorious "living forces of the nation", to collaborate with the bourgeoisie in politics and economics is to bolster a bourgeois order which has shattered once and for all. It means helping it to carry on for years or even decades, borne on the stooping shoulders of the working class. ...

The Menshevik conception of the present historical process determines the whole policy of Menshevik social-democracy. It determines their attitude to the war and to its liquidation, it determines their defencism... The upshot is that the revolution is subordinated to, and almost suffocated by, the requirements of defence. The bourgeois arguments of the Kadet party and others on the war are identical almost to the letter with those of our socialist-defencists. To continue the war on the conditions created by Nicholas and the ruling classes is to continue to strengthen the position of the bourgeoisie, both Russian and West European. We cannot deny that the Mensheviks are true to their tactics, which are in complete accord with the basis of their programme.

But it might well be asked, what are we, the Party of Socialist-Revolutionaries, doing here? The party is faithfully following the tactics advanced by the Mensheviks, it very frequently votes for Menshevik resolutions, and they are *always* united, the party and the Mensheviks – a single voice, a single organ of the Soviet majority. There is some kind of tragic misunderstanding here, fraught with dangerous consequences.

The Party of Socialist-Revolutionaries is at the forefront of the social revolution. The implementation of its programme will destroy one of the firmest pillars of the present order (landownership), it will violate one of the most sacred principles of the bourgeois order – that of private property. It is not only in the future that it will be an overt and powerful enemy of the bourgeois classes. It is not an enemy in preparation. It is their enemy now, in its immediate tasks. Let it stand before the bourgeoisie openly.

Source: *Nash Put'*, No. 1, August 1917
Published in Ya V Leont'ev (compiler), *Partiya levykh sotsialistov-revolyutsionerov, dokumenty i materialy, t. 1, Iyul' 1917 g.–may 1918 g.*, ROSSPEN, Moscow, 2000. pp. 52–54.

The much smaller People's Socialist Party (NSs) – a very moderate group whose main support was among the intelligentsia – had also been considering their relations with the other socialist groups. They had concluded, like the SRs, that differentiation of the parties was an essential prerequisite for unification. At their first all-Russia congress in June 1917, they did indeed merge with the Trudoviks, a very small support group for the narodnik-inclined deputies in the Duma. But the enthusiasm for merging with the SRs was waning, not least because it was fairly clear they would be swamped by the much larger body. Venedikt Myakotin's survey of the political landscape gives a good account of the overall NS approach, as well as some astute comments on the other parties of the left. At the same time, it is not hard to see why the NSs were completely marginalised in the turmoil and growing polarisation of Russian politics in 1917.

Document 14. V A Myakotin's report on the People's Socialists' attitude to other socialist parties

21 June 1917

...I would like to say a few words about our own party, about our tactics. The People's Socialist Party has always worked for, and called for, those things in which it is both able and willing to take part itself. This was one of the factors that gave rise to the party. Other political parties often advance slogans without considering their feasibility. ... This often happens when political life is underdeveloped. *I* call on others to rise up, to strike, to withhold their taxes etc., but won't do anything *myself* - and these words just remain hanging in the air.

In countries which are more developed politically they are aware of this. Countries like Hungary or Finland can serve as examples of how to conduct politics properly. We start from the position that the party should only take decisions that it is in a position to fulfil. This tactical line has always distinguished us from the other socialist parties. We are tiny in comparison to the other socialist parties, we have few members, but we stick to our line. As for our relationship to other parties, there is also a deep gulf between our party and the non-socialist parties. We have a definite ideal, but we do not envisage attaining it miraculously, in just one bound. We see the transition to it as a series of steps, one after the other, taken by the organised forces of the people. We must constantly look around and ask ourselves whether a given step is taking us towards a socialist society. Non-socialists are not concerned about this. But this does not mean that we are opponents of the non-socialist parties at every turn, everywhere, and on everything. The realm of socialism is a long way off, and there is a whole series of tasks that non-socialists could also set themselves. Of all the non-socialist parties we can only speak of the Constitutional Democrats. We should take stock of the fact that a significant number of rightist elements have now gathered in that party, but we should not forget that it also contains genuine elements of non-socialist democracy. We can find people in its ranks who are trying to involve the masses in building the life of the nation. They should not all be lumped together under the general heading of "bourgeoisie", and it makes no sense to renounce any businesslike contacts with them once and for all.

...There is no one, single [social-democratic] party. There are many interpretations of it, and many contradictory tendencies. There are sometimes deep-rooted reasons for these factional differences. Overall, we have little in common with the Mensheviks. But for all the great differences in our programmes, we have much in common with them in terms of tactics. They are pure Marxists. They view the position of Russia completely differently from us. To them the peasantry is a bourgeoisie, the only motive force is the proletariat, and the social revolution can only come through the power and dictatorship of the proletariat. We have a completely different conception, but on tactical questions we often find ourselves hand in hand with them. They are distinguished by their serious approach to political and social questions, they think things through and remain true to the socialist programme. The basic tactical line of the Mensheviks is more thought out, scientific and socialist than those of other social-democratic groups. But we must be more firm and courageous in our resistance to the Bolsheviks, while the Mensheviks sometimes allow themselves to be led by them.

The Bolsheviks have moved a long way from Marxist theory – they advocate giving the land over for use by all the people.

It is hard to determine what we are dealing with here. Their tactic is to take all the revolutionary slogans to the extreme. For example, they demand the overthrow of the Provisional Government and the transfer of all power to the Soviets of Workers' and Soldiers' Deputies. What nonsense is this, to give all power to those who do not want it? ... The basic element of their tactics is violence. This is Jacobinism of the worst type, but not socialism. There are some clever people and socialists amongst them, but their general line is not socialist, and is mixed with Black Hundredism. If we were forced to choose, we would even prefer the Kadets to the Bolsheviks. ...

Let us now look at the narodnik parties.

When the revolution broke out and the SRs emerged from the underground, we tried merging with them. We thought we could reconsider our programme together, so that each of us could find our place within it, without feeling suppressed or oppressed. At first the SRs agreed. Each group even selected a delegation of three people. The first two meetings were quite successful, but then the Bolshevik current within the SRs began to get stronger, and their Moscow conference rejected the idea of unification. After this conference *Delo naroda* changed its approach, and a hostile attitude towards the NSs and the Trudoviks began to grow and gather strength. Nonetheless, there are people within the SRs who are very close to us. But, although they are close to us on questions of programme and tactics, they remain organisationally linked to the SR party. That is the *Volya naroda* group.

The final narodnik group is the Trudovik party.

The underground SR party gathered one set of elements in its ranks, the NSs - another, and the Trudoviks - a third group. We had wanted to merge all these currents, all these elements and all these temperaments, but now it is just a question of merging with the Trudoviks. The very fact that we cannot explain to the electorate what the difference is between us means that we need to merge...

Source: A V Sypchenko, K N Morozov (compilers), *Trudovaya Narodno-Sotsialisticheskaya Partiya: dokumenty i materialy*, ROSSPEN, Moscow, 2003, pp. 255 - 257.

On the very far left of narodism, at the point where it almost shaded into anarchism, stood the Union of SR-Maximalists (SSRM). This group was just reconstituting itself in 1917, having burnt itself out in a blaze of armed struggle in 1906-07. Its nucleus in 1917 was of old Maximalists returned from exile, but the SSRM was reconstructed in the summer largely from groups of leftists splitting from the main SR organisation in various places. Later on, the SSRM was overshadowed by the growing left within the SR party itself, which formally split away in November 1917 to become the Left SR party. The SSRM did not produce a programme until October, but the rules devised in June reflect its characteristic combination of radicalism and a certain vagueness.

Document 15. Rules of the SR-Maximalist Organisation, adopted at the conference of the Petrograd and Kronstadt Initiative Groups of SR-Maximalists

11 June 1917

1. Only a socialist and revolutionary, that is, a person who consciously strives for the establishment of a workers' system by means of a revolution of the working people organised around its Soviets, may become a member of the organisation.

2. The members are united in their common view of the current revolution as a social revolution, by their firm desire to organise all the forces interested in its success and to find viable ways to total class victory - to a workers' republic, where power, the land, the factories and capital will be in the hands of the people.

3. Members come together in factories, mills, villages, military units, forming groups of people who know one another well and trust one another.

4. Its executive organs are comprised of representatives of factory, peasants' and soldiers' (company and command) groups.

5. People whose position does not fit them into any of the above groups will form a strictly organised auxiliary group, whose members will only have an advisory voice in the executive organs (point 4).

The main goals of the organisation:

1. Actively to assist the working people to unite in a fraternal, non-partisan way around their class representation, that is, around the Soviets of Peasants', Workers' and Soldiers' Deputies and around the factory committees.

2. To elaborate and propagate its views.

The adoption of these rules means that:

1. The organisation will not accept people who are unworthy, not sober, act thoughtlessly or are conciliatory towards the ruling classes.

2. The organisation does not permit slogans or actions leading to discord and hostility between workers.

3. The organisation does not permit any seizures, armed uprisings or terrorist acts carried out against the wishes of the local Soviet of Workers', Peasants' and Soldiers' Deputies.

4. The organisation stands for a real transfer of power to the Soviets of Peasants', Workers' and Soldiers' Deputies. Commissions of expert specialists should work under their direction and supervision.

5. The organisation takes a critical but impartial attitude to the actions of central government, whether it be a coalition, a group of people belonging to socialist parties or even a government in Soviet guise.

6. On the question of the social structure: the organisation does not adopt plans which are based merely on theoretical constructions or good intentions, rather than on a study of life and the actual situation.

7. On the question of tactics in the revolution, the organisation sees the main strength in local mass organisations. It rejects the view that the outcome of the revolution can depend solely on some central authority (the government, the Constituent Assembly etc.)

8. On the national question, the organisation recognises the right of every citizen to workers' self-determination, that is, to the realisation of complete national freedom, not distorted by capitalist or gentry provocation. The final formulation of this principle is to be left to the first all-Russian conference.

9. On the question of the war: we support the principle of peace without annexations or indemnities with the right of peoples to self-determination. In addition we demand the establishment of a European Federation of Free Peoples (a United States of Europe) and the abolition of standing armies. The organisation will not accept, on the one hand, supporters of a separate peace with the bourgeois-feudal governments of the German coalition, or on the other, persons recognising treaties with the bourgeois governments of the Allied and neutral states.

10. On the question of trade unions and labour exchanges, the organisation sees their role as nothing more than providing statistical and technical services to the working class, under the supervision and control of the Soviets of Workers' Deputies and the factory committees.

The organisation allows freedom of opinion both in regard to the philosophical foundation of its programme and tactics, and on all specific questions within the limits laid down by the basic organisation.

These rules have been adopted by the conference of the Petrograd and Kronstadt Initiative Groups of SR-Maximalists.

Originally published in G A Rivkin, *Po puti k Trudovoy Respublike i sotsializmu*, Petrograd, 1917.
Source: D B Pavlov, compiler, *Soyuz Eserov-Maksimalistov: dokumenty, publitsistika, 1906 - 1924 gg.*, ROSSPEN, Moscow, 2002, pp. 100 - 101.

Alongside the familiar divisions into left and right, Russian politics increasingly fragmented along national lines in the course of 1917. In the Ukraine, for example, alongside the all-Russia SR party which operated in many Ukrainian towns and cities, a separate Ukrainian Party of Socialist-Revolutionaries was formed from various local groups, and held its founding congress in May 1917. One of the prominent people who joined the new UPSR was the historian M S Hrushevsky, whose political activities up to then had been identified far more with Ukrainian nationalism than narodnik socialism. In this resolution from the founding congress of the USPR, social and economic demands are very much secondary to national demands.

Document 16. Resolution of the founding congress of the Ukrainian Party of Socialist-Revolutionaries

4 - 5 April 1917

1. On the question of autonomy and federation:

a) At a time when great creative endeavours are taking place among the free peoples of Russia, the founding congress of the UPSR recognises that the greatest need of the Ukrainian people is the implementation of wide-ranging national and territorial autonomy for the Ukraine, with guarantees for the rights of national minorities. A Ukrainian Constituent Council should be convened urgently to work out the forms and bases of this autonomy, and to prepare the elections to the All-Russia Constituent Assembly for the Ukrainian people and the other peoples on the territory of the Ukraine.

b) If the Russian government hinders the convocation of a Ukrainian Constituent Council by force at all, or makes any attempt to exert pressure with the help of force, the Party of Ukrainian Socialist-Revolutionaries will regard this as a continuation of the imperialist policy of predation and oppression that the Muscovite Tsars and the Russian Emperors pursued towards the Ukraine.

c) At the same time the congress considers that the best type of structure for the Russian state would be a federative-democratic republic, and the UPSR will work for this at the All-Russia Constituent Assembly.

2. On the question of our attitude to the Provisional Government:

a) The party supports the Provisional Government in its work, insofar as it defends the interests of the working people.

b) The party demands that the Provisional Government make a declaration on its attitude to Ukrainian autonomy.

3. On the question of the war:

a) The party looks upon the war as a war for the freedom of the peoples of Russia, and urges that the Provisional Government conclude peace with the warring powers, so long as the governments of the hostile powers renounce annexations and encroachments upon the freedom of the peoples of Russia.

b) Welcoming the Provisional Government's declaration on ending the war without annexations or reparations, the party urges the Government to take a further step in this direction and announce peace terms consistent with the demands of democracy. Only such a step will enable the democracies of the warring powers to exert the necessary pressure on their governments to compel these governments to negotiate the speediest end to the war.

c) The Ukrainian SRs insist that the nations of Europe without states should be able to decide their own destinies at the peace conference, including their national self determination.

d) The Ukrainian SRs address their appeal to the revolutionary masses of the warring powers to struggle actively against the predatory policies of their governments.

e) Believing that the Ukrainian soldiers, spread around various military units, will be unable fully to express their will at the Constituent Assembly elections if these elections take place during wartime, the UPSR calls for Ukrainian servicemen to be concentrated in distinct regiments.

This resolution was adopted at the founding congress in Kiev.

Source: document reproduced on Kiev University history website: www.history.univ.kiev.ua/ukrbooks/doc1900.html

Mariya Aleksandrovna Spiridonova

VII. Peasants, Food and Land Reform

An agrarian programme which articulated the desires of much of Russia's peasantry was the SRs' political trump card. During the period of reaction between 1907 and 1917, the SRs' rural organisation had all but collapsed, but after the fall of the Tsar, they turned their attention to the villages again. The leading figures in rural SR groups often tended to be from the village intelligentsia (schoolteachers, zemstvo employees and so on), but there is no doubt that the party quickly regained its mass support among the peasants, which proved much more resilient throughout 1917 than its support in the cities and among the soldiers.

SRs dominated the peasant soviets, village committees and other organisations that sprang up after February. The resolutions, statements and appeals these bodies issued in the name of the peasants often followed a template produced by a local party organisation, and also included demands which were probably far from the real concerns of the peasants who approved them. The following resolution of Znamenskaya *volost'* (group of villages) in Tambov province is typical of the genre. In this instance, its politics reflect the right wing of the SR party, and its wording is almost completely identical to a resolution of the citizens of Pereksinskaya *volost'* nearby. It is also noteworthy that the 35 literate and 70 illiterate peasants who put their names to this resolution were, without exception, male.

Document 17. Resolution of the citizens of Znamenskaya *volost'*

16 April 1917

We, citizens of the villages of Znamenskaya *volost'* in Tambov *uezd*, Tambov *guberniya*, assembled on 16 April 1917 at a *volost'* meeting with 105 people present. We discussed the questions of the present moment and unanimously resolved to inform the Provisional Government and the Tambov *uezd* and *guberniya* committees of the following:

1) In order to secure the freedom of the Russian people and all peoples of the world, the war should be carried on to a victorious conclusion and the complete destruction of Prussian militarism and imperialism.

2) We consider the only suitable state structure for the Russian people to be a democratic republic.

3) Distribution of land to citizen peasants from a fund made up of land owned by the Tsar and his family, private landowners, monasteries etc.

a) Monastery cash holdings should be confiscated by the state.

b) This distribution should be based on the principle that everyone should be offered a holding that he can work himself along with his family.

Until all the above land goes into the state fund there must be a strict watch on the area sown and the integrity of forests, woods and other land resources.

4) Universal compulsory general and professional education free of charge.

Mitrofan Kocherygin [and 104 others]

Archive source: State Archive of Tambov *Oblast'* (GATO), f. R-1, op. 1, d. 3, ll. 19-20
Published on: www.tstu.ru/win/kultur/other/istr/html10.htm

SR influence among the peasantry was demonstrated at the 1st All-Russia Congress of Soviets of Peasant Deputies, from 4 – 28 May 1917. Of the 1167 delegates registered, 537 identified themselves as SRs, compared to 90 Mensheviks and just 9 Bolsheviks. The executive committee elected by the congress, which claimed to speak for Russia's peasants, consisted almost entirely of prominent SR politicians, few of whom had much recent experience of working in fields. (Professional politicians also dominated the leaderships elected by workers' and soldiers' soviet congresses in 1917.)

The whole question of agriculture presented a series of intractable problems in 1917. Food shortages and rising prices had been one of the major grievances behind the street demonstrations which helped topple the Tsar in February and March. A reliable food supply was essential for maintaining the army as well as the towns and cities. The Provisional Government had introduced a state monopoly in grain purchasing at the end of March, and had fixed purchase prices, in order to protect the budget and lessen inflationary pressures. But the prices of the goods the peasants wanted to buy – where these were available at all – were rising ever faster. Selling at state prices meant that peasants were increasingly producing at a loss, and being paid in banknotes that depreciated in value from day to day.

In this situation, the promise of the long-awaited land reform, the source of the SRs' popularity in the countryside, could only serve to make things worse. Some of the richer peasants and landowners (i.e. the people who could produce a surplus for sale) were disinclined to sow their fields where they feared they would no longer own them by harvest time.

Part-elected land committees had been created by the Provisional Government to prepare for the agrarian reform; they existed alongside peasant soviets and similar rural bodies. But the complexity of the impending reform, and the need to ensure a harvest in 1917 meant that the land committees could not do much in the short term to redistribute the land, even where they had the power to do so.

Annoyed at this stalling, in certain places the more impatient peasants began to organise their own local land reforms. This spontaneous peasant movement grew in the course of 1917. But the redistributions they effected were far from invariably rational or just, especially given that many peasants were absent from their villages, in the armed forces or in war work. In the very worst cases, they amounted to little more than looting.

The SR leadership wanted a model land reform in Russia, enacted by a democratically-elected Constituent Assembly, to redistribute the land in a transparently fair and just fashion. In the meantime, however, someone, somewhere, had to sow the crops for 1917. At the congress, the right-wing SR Semyon Maslov appealed to the peasants to show patience and restraint, arguing that the land reform was a foregone conclusion.

Document 18. S L Maslov: On land usage up to the Constituent Assembly

16 May 1917

The revolution has put the practical solution of the land question onto the agenda. The satisfaction of the working peasantry's land requirements is no longer just an age-old dream. The time has come to implement the land reform in reality, legally, in full, across the whole country. And we must recognise that the direction the land reform will take has already been decided by the revolutionary will of the working people.

The call for all the land to become the property of the whole people, to be used by those who work it, has today been taken up by the widest masses of the people. There is no force that can prevent land holding being reorganised on this basis.

The peasantry of all Russia, united and organised, has taken the fate of the land reform into its own hands.

The land reform consists of two parts. One is to devise the requisite land law and set out the corresponding rules for land use. The other is to implement this new land law. But, in addition, another new task has arisen.

As everyone appreciates, the new land law can only be devised by an all-national Constituent Assembly. The full and final settlement of the land question is the Constituent Assembly's task. But at the same time we all understand the trouble, losses, and oppression the working peasantry suffers under the present agrarian structure, based on private property in land. And this presents us with a specific problem: what should we do in the meantime, before the Constituent Assembly? Should all the current unjust relations which flow from this structure be left intact and untouched, or can some changes and corrections be introduced?

Life itself dictates that ... we cannot leave everything just as it was. And so, the third aspect to the land reform is preparatory. It concerns the actions and measures that have to be taken in the area of agrarian policy prior to the Constituent Assembly....

The first question we face is that of preventative measures.

In this case we have in mind the buying and selling of land, mortgages, gifts and so on. Landowners might engage in these sorts of deals in order to exercise their property rights on the eve of the land reform. We hear that landowners sometimes try to sell or mortgage their land to foreign nationals. Even if deals of this sort present no danger in the final analysis to the impending reform, they do present unnecessary complications. The same goes for any use of Stolypin's legislation against the peasant commune: consolidating commune land and hiving portions off. All those sorts of deals should be stopped once and for all. This requires, in addition to local public opinion, appropriate orders by the Provisional Government...

Let us now proceed to the question of land seizures.

It seems that in certain areas, primarily where there are no peasant organisations, peasants are trying to exercise their right to the land by seizing the neighbouring landlord's land on their own account. The question arises as to how far that is expedient.

We can see ... how unevenly stocks of land are distributed around the regions and provinces of Russia. But the same unevenness exists within *uezda* and even *volosti*. Each of us will have seen many times how a large estate will have several hamlets and villages grouped around it, usually renting land from that landowner, while at the same time other villages are far away from any major reserves of land. It is not difficult to imagine the difficulties for any correct solution to the land question if each province or region stakes a claim to its own exclusive lands, and seizes them for itself. It is not difficult to predict what will happen if individual villages of peasants seize the land of the neighbouring landowners, leaving other peasants without land. Matters will be even worse if these seizures are carried out by individuals or groups of peasants. And more often than not seizures take place in exactly this way.

Peasants often try to seize land in the hope that if they manage to sow it, they will be able to keep it. But only those peasant households that have enough workers and horses can manage that. Families without horses, families with few workers or who have members serving in the army are in no position to use seizure to secure land for themselves. It is therefore clear that it can be advantageous for the stronger peasants and even those with more land already, but not for those who need land most of all.

In addition, there are two other considerations which speak against land seizures by individual groups of peasants.

Initially, in the first days of the revolution, when the rumour went round the army amongst the soldiers that land was being redistributed at home, many got back home as fast as they could for fear of being left out, which increased the level of desertion. Finally, land seizures run the risk of reducing the area sown. There have been cases where peasants, having seized the landowner's land, have either sown it poorly or thinly, or have left their own land unsown. At this time, when our country needs food so urgently, such a state of affairs is completely impermissible.

Some might object to all this: what? Are you telling us to leave everything just as it is, after we have put up with landlord property for so long? But certainly not all the peasants will think that way. For example, we have a resolution from the peasant deputies in the 1st Army. It contains the following passage on this question: "The final resolution of the question must be left to the Constituent Assembly, and until that question is resolved the land committees should a) ensure that all derelict and unused land is ploughed and sown by local peasants to ensure sufficient grain for the army and the whole population; b) take charge of both land

and forest resources, without having any right to appropriate, sell or mortgage them. All land which has already been sown should remain untouched, and in general no damaging action at all should be done to anyone else's land. All disorders and disturbances that may arise should be resisted as strongly as possible."

These points from that resolution display a sense of great statesmanship. The peasants know and understand that the land is not going to slip away from them, but they can foresee that in order to resolve the land question correctly, time, and a great deal of work is required....

...During this war the landowners' farms have shown a fall in the area sown. In the current year, for a variety of reasons further falls may be expected. This is completely at variance with the present needs of the country. In view of the acuteness of the food situation decisive measures must be taken to ensure there is no undersowing. Therefore, wherever there is arable land and meadowland, no matter to whom it belongs ... whose owners will not or cannot use it in the current sowing period, then that land should be given over on certain conditions to those who want to sow it. ...

Land not being used by its owners should preferably be rented out only for growing grain or hay, in the first instance to artels of poor peasants, then to middle peasants, with only the remainder being rented to the well-off.

These are the basic principles for interim land use until the Constituent Assembly. ...

Source: *Delo naroda*, No. 54, 20 May 1917.
Published in N D Erofeev, compiler, *Partiya sotisialistov-revolyutsionerov. Dokumenty i materialy*, Vol. 3 part 1, ROSSPEN, Moscow, 2000, pp. 127 - 132.

Twelve days earlier, just before Viktor Chernov took his post as agriculture minister, the young SR economist Nikolay Kondrat'ev had spelt out the problems facing Russia with regard to food supply.

Document 19. N D Kondrat'ev: Supplying the villages and the food crisis

4 May 1917

Messages and resolutions from peasants on the food question are coming in from all sides. In these resolutions the peasants affirm that they will supply grain at the prices fixed, but only on condition that industry is also controlled and the countryside is supplied with the necessary consumer goods and equipment.

So, the peasants are expressing their willingness to come to the aid of the motherland, but are setting certain conditions.

These resolutions and conditions contain a profound living truth. Supplying the countryside with the goods and equipment it needs is an urgent, acute question which cannot be put off. It is vitally important not only from the peasants' point of view, but also from the point of view of the state. The stability and durability of the new state order is now dependent upon the stability of the countryside and the productivity of agriculture. The new order will only survive if it can avoid starvation in the army, the towns, and the grain-consuming villages.

Moreover, the war has inflicted deep wounds on agriculture and its productivity.

The countryside has given the armed forces 50% of its male workforce. It has given up an enormous quantity of draught animals. And at the same time the countryside is deprived of the chance to replace its equipment, deprived of even the minimum necessary quantity of consumer goods.

The war has struck at the very heart of the countryside, draining it of its material productive forces. And we understand why it is that in its resolutions the peasantry does not complain about prices or money, but mainly about material supplies to the villages. This reflects both the great wisdom of the peasants, and their most pressing needs.

Supplying the countryside with fuel, goods and equipment is not only an urgent matter, but one which is closely linked with solving the food crisis.

However, there are immense difficulties with sorting out supplies: there is not even enough metal for military needs, there is a shortage of cloth and other industrial products.

The old order was criminally negligent towards the countryside. All the time that the shortages of industrial products and equipment were growing with dizzying speed, the old authorities did not take the requisite measures to regulate the production of these goods or to plan their distribution. The whole burden of regulation lay on agriculture, which also suffered the major share of unsatisfied needs.

By this spring, only 1.5% of the existing orders placed with our domestic ironworking industry had been fulfilled. But, despite the feebleness of that branch of industry, it was not until June or July 1916 that the government placed large-scale orders for agricultural machinery, equipment and twine in America, England and Sweden. 108370 machines and 900000 puds* of twine were ordered. Of that total, 61599 machines and 515961 puds of twine have been dispatched. But most of them are still in transit. Only 7958 machines and 300000 puds of twine have actually arrived. In other words, the goods are going to arrive too late. Transport difficulties are partly to blame, but to a great extent it is the negligence of the former government.

The new government, of course, feels the needs of the countryside acutely, and work picked up when it came to power. Through economies it has released a certain quantity of metal for agriculture, which had previously been intended for defence work. It has put agricultural implements into the top category for priority

---

* 1 pud = 16.38 kilograms or 36.1 lb.

freight, it has given local government bodies the right to requisition agricultural machinery left in railway sidings without documentation, etc. The government has just now placed a significant new order abroad for agricultural implements.

At the same time, the government has paid attention to providing agriculture with workers. It has placed a significant number of prisoners of war at its disposal, certain military units, and, finally, although this is less important, student brigades. Overall, this will provide agriculture with one million extra workers.

Matters are worse regarding price controls and distribution of consumer goods to the countryside – cloth, paraffin, paper and so on. The government has only just started sorting out this question. But life will not wait. It demands decisive action.

For some reason government measures generally seem to display dilatoriness, but in this case it is particularly apparent. Is the government afraid to regulate large-scale capitalist enterprise more firmly?

Whatever the case, even with the most decisive and brilliant measures, the matter of supplying the countryside with goods cannot be solved in a couple of weeks. If there is no iron and no cloth, if nothing was done about this earlier, they cannot be created from words and desires. We all need to recognise and understand this.

At the same time, famine is approaching, and the struggle against it cannot be put off for one day, nor even for one hour.

So, we find ourselves in a tragic situation. Famine is knocking at the door. And the peasants, tormented and fatigued, quite reasonably demand that the countryside be supplied with the goods it needs, and only agree to give grain on that condition. But supplying the countryside is a long process, and if the peasants stick firmly to their position, then we will be facing further food riots. And who can tell whether they will shake the new order to its foundations, just as they shook the old order?

Where is the way out? In our view, there is only one, and we will state it directly: the countryside must give us grain. It has made its demands, stated its conditions, but it must not carry out its threats now, immediately. Because that is impossible! It threatens to ruin our country's freedom, its well-being, and, thereby the well-being of the countryside itself.

The voice of the countryside should be heard, and decisive and effective measures to supply the countryside should be taken immediately.

But the village must save the motherland. It made many sacrifices under the old regime. And we are sure that it will find the strength for further great sacrifices, but these will be sacrifices, we believe, for the happiness of our liberated country.

Source: *Volya naroda*, 4 May 1917
Published in V M Bondarenko et al., compilers, *N D Kondrat'ev. Izbrannye sochineniya*, Ekonomika, Moscow, 1993, pp. 313 – 315.

Thus, by the late spring of 1917, the SR leadership had staked a great deal of its political credit on the promise of good things in the future. Its supporters in the army were urged to fight on, on the promise of a democratic peace without annexations or indemnities. Its supporters in the countryside were urged to show restraint in challenging the existing agrarian order, on the promise of a truly just land reform enacted by the Constituent Assembly, and to carry on providing grain at fixed prices, on the promise that the government would try to improve the supply of industrial goods. Viktor Chernov had taken the post of agriculture minister, raising hopes that he and the other socialist ministers would push the government into more radical action in the interests of peasants, workers and soldiers. Over the coming months, as Russia's military and economic situation continued to deteriorate, patience gave way to impatience, hopes gave way to frustration and disillusionment, and the SR party itself began to unravel.

Nikolay Dmitrievich Kondrat'ev

51

VIII. The June Offensive and the July Demonstrations

A fatal weakness of "revolutionary defencism" as a policy was that there was no clear military stance associated with it: it made sense only if peace were more or less imminent. In rejecting the idea of a separate peace with Germany, the revolutionary defencist majority in the Soviets committed Russia to continuing the war. But in also rejecting the notion of "war to a victorious conclusion" when all the other belligerent states still had their sights set on victory, the policy put Russia in the absurd position of fighting, but not in order to win. Kerensky, in his new post of war minister, appreciated that marking time on the front was having a corrosive effect on the army. He therefore organised an offensive on the South-Western front, commanded by General A A Brusilov, starting on 18 June 1917. He toured the front, rallying the troops, and sent enthusiastic reports to Petrograd about the initial successes of the offensive.

Document 20. Kerensky's report from the South-Western front

To-day is a day of triumph for the revolution. On the 18th June the Russian Revolutionary Army began the attack with tremendous enthusiasm, and so proved to Russia and to the rest of the world its absolute devotion to the cause of the revolution and its love for liberty and for the fatherland.

Contemptuously leaving behind them at home the unimportant group of cowards, the free Russian warriors prove by their offensive the existence of a new discipline resting on their sense of duty as citizens. Whatever may happen now, this day has made an end of the malicious and slanderous attacks on the organisations of the Russian army built upon a democratic basis. I urgently request permission to hand over to the regiments who took part in the battles of the 18th June the red flags of the revolution in the name of the liberated people, the red flags which even now, during the battle, are being waved by the attacking regiments on their own initiative. I also ask that all regiments who opened the offensive be styled "Regiment of the 18th June".

Kerensky

Published in W Astrov et al, eds, *An Illustrated History of the Russian Revolution*, Martin Lawrence, London, 1928, p. 175. (Translated by Freda Utley.)

The "unimportant group of cowards" that so irked Kerensky were the anti-war demonstrators who hi-jacked the demonstration called by the Petrograd Soviet on 18 June in support of the Provisional Government and the offensive. At the Petrograd Soviet, Kerensky's fellow SR minister, Chernov, tried to defend the offensive, but in terms which suggested that his heart was not really in it. Chernov's hopes for peace at this time, like those of many internationalist socialists, were invested in a proposed conference in Stockholm of European socialist parties. This "socialist conference", to which Chernov referred, would have brought socialists from all sides together to explore ways to achieve a just peace. It was eventually scuppered, in part, by the British

Liberal Prime Minister Lloyd George, who refused to grant passports to the British delegation.

Document 21. Report of V M Chernov's speech at the Petrograd Soviet

20 June 1917

The speaker ... examined the accusations levelled against the Provisional Government regarding its foreign policy.

"In criticising the government for its dilatoriness and half-heartedness, they propose decisive measures like presenting an ultimatum to the Allies and declaring war on the whole world. But an ultimatum would not bring peace nearer; it would delay it. Our trouble is that the most backward country has taken the most advanced position.

"The power of the democracy in the West is growing, but it is growing slowly. By trying to force the issue we will just bring down an avalanche of hatred upon our own comrades abroad.

"We must not push them, we must offer the socialists abroad the chance to give battle to the imperialists as and when they find it possible and necessary."

Comrade Chernov continued: "Russia has already resolved the question of Poland, but Germany has not yet done so..."

(From the audience: "What about Finland? Ukraine?")

"There is a Ukrainian question, there is a Finnish question, but I do not believe that we have all lost so much faith in revolutionary Russia as to think that they will not be resolved at the Constituent Assembly.

"Our faith in revolutionary Russia gives us the conviction that we are not taking on any war aims other than those we have already proclaimed, and the offensive will not change them.

"Maybe the offensive is a mistake? But, if we do not make a move ourselves, we would just be waiting until Hindenburg's reactionary armies struck and smashed Russia's revolutionary troops.

"We have chosen the lesser of two evils, but we are not going to run to the other extreme of war until victory. We will carry on repeating to our comrades abroad: help us end this terrible war, enough of this bloodshed, do what we did, overthrow your yoke, as we overthrew ours.

"The way out is not through fraternisation at the front, but through internationalist fraternisation at the socialist conference, which alone can save the country.

"Our offensive is a heavy cross to bear. It is especially heavy for our comrades at the front, and therefore we propose to send them our fraternal, revolutionary, internationalist greetings."

Source: *Delo naroda*, No. 80, 21 June 1917.
Published in N D Erofeev, compiler, *Partiya sotisialistov-revolyutsionerov. Dokumenty i materialy*, Vol. 3 part 1, ROSSPEN, Moscow, 2000, p. 668.

We do not know how Chernov's "fraternal, revolutionary, internationalist greetings" were received at the front, but they did not prevent the offensive from faltering after a few days. A German counterattack more than made good the Central Powers' initial losses. Desertion from the Russian army increased. As the futility of continuing the war became increasingly apparent, anti-war sentiment, and a mood of frustration and disillusionment, grew, not least among those who were expected to do the fighting.

On 2 July another crisis hit the Provisional Government, as the liberal Kadet ministers resigned in protest at concessions made to Ukrainian separatism. To add to the chaos, on 3 – 5 July, large, disorderly, armed demonstrations of sailors from the Kronstadt naval base, soldiers and workers took to the streets of Petrograd. Their demands were somewhat confused, but included Soviet power, the removal of the government, and an end to the war. There were some exchanges of gunfire, with casualties. Prominent Bolsheviks had been closely involved in organising the demonstrations, although whether they represented an abortive attempt to take power at that time remains unclear. One notable incident of the "July Days" was the seizure of Chernov, who had been sent out by the Petrograd Soviet to address the crowd, by a group of angry sailors, and his rescue from an uncertain fate by Trotsky.

The reactions to the demonstrations within the SR party show how divided the party had become at this time. The official line of the Petrograd committee was condemnatory:

Document 22. "Comrades Soldiers and Workers!" Appeal of the Petrograd SR committee

4 July 1917

The authoritative organs of the whole Russian people, the Soviets of Workers', Soldiers' and Peasants' Deputies, stand guard for liberty and the revolution. Today, they are deciding the question of the fate of the Provisional Government, following the resignation of the members of the Kadet party. The whole working people awaits this decision with impatience, as it should give a powerful new impetus to the development of the Russian revolution and the struggle for peace. However, a certain part of the population and the garrison in Petrograd has given vent to its impatience; in spite of the decision of all the authoritative organs of Russian democracy and the appeals from all the revolutionary socialist parties, it has gone out onto the streets bearing arms. However much the democracy would like to see all power in the hands of the Soviets of Workers', Soldiers' and Peasants' Deputies, this behaviour is *impermissible*. It disorganises the forces of revolution, it leads to unnecessary and criminal bloodshed, and undermines the power and influence of those revolutionary organs that you yourselves elected, that were elected by millions of working people in the towns and villages.

Comrades, our strength lies only in organised revolutionary discipline. Unite around the Soviets of Workers', Soldiers' and Peasants' Deputies. The fate of the revolution is in your hands.

Published in N D Erofeev, compiler, *Partiya sotisialistov-revolyutsionerov. Dokumenty i materialy*, Vol. 3 part 1, ROSSPEN, Moscow, 2000, p. 673

However, there were left-wing supporters of the SRs among the demonstrators, and the "Socialist-Revolutionary-Internationalists", the faction within the party which was to form the nucleus of the Left SR breakaway in November, issued a proclamation shortly after the events justifying the demonstrations.

Document 23. Proclamation of the Organising Committee and VTsIK Faction of the Socialist-Revolutionary-Internationalists

July 1917

In struggle you will find your rights!

Comrade workers and soldiers!

By the will of the revolutionary people, the question of completing the establishment of people's power is now ready to be settled finally and unambiguously. The demand to transfer all power to the soviets of workers', peasants' and soldiers' deputies has been supported by the workers and soldiers who came out onto the streets.

Their voice should be heeded. This is not just the voice of Petersburg. The Petersburg proletariat and the "regiments of the 27th of February" were called upon to speak for the whole of Russia during the decisive days [of February 1917]. From the first days of the revolution all Russia accorded this right to the Petersburg Soviet of Workers' and Soldiers' Deputies. The claims of the bourgeoisie, that Petersburg is not only not in step with the rest of Russia but stands against it, should be indignantly rejected as unworthy slander. We have heard this at "private gatherings of the State Duma" from the Third of June Duma Deputies,* who have been thrown off the path of Russia's history, but such talk is not compatible with democracy. Petersburg has been in the vanguard of the Russian revolution, and it remains at its post as the guardian of the people's freedom. And if its sensitivity, its alertness, occasionally obliges it to raise its voice impatiently, on its own initiative, then democracy will not blame it for that.

The people can sense the closeness of its long awaited freedom - a real freedom, a social freedom, the triumph of emancipated labour. The people cannot accept that once again, as so often before in history, this freedom, bought with the people's blood in our great February uprising, is just a spectre, a momentary glimpse of sunlight. For this reason the people constantly and intensely watches the government's every step, every turn of the rudder of the ship of state. The experience of coalition with the bourgeoisie in the "coalition" Provisional

---

* "Third of June Duma" - on 3 June 1907 the government, exasperated by the Russian people's persistent tendency to elect left-wing deputies to the State Duma, imposed a new, very unequal, electoral law which gave much greater weight to propertied elements.

Government was, and indeed should have been, a hard test for the revolutionary democracy. For day after day, step after step, we saw the revolution being diverted from its straight path, the path of social freedom. We had embarked on this path after long years of heroic struggle on our own for the emancipation of labour, for land and freedom. Instead, the revolution has gone down the winding path of compromise politics. This path leads not to the vista of free social construction, but into the blind alley of a bourgeois republic, in which freedom will once again be a mere spectre, and labour, the highest, best and only human good, will bend as before under the yoke of capitalism.

Naturally, as this has become clear, there has been mounting concern within the ranks of revolutionary democracy. It has finally broken out in an active form as open protest. Revolution does not tolerate compromise. As long as the revolution lives, any compromise can only complicate the creative process, the life of the upsurge of renewal. But the revolution is still alive, whatever its gravediggers may say...

The All-Russian Executive Committee should heed the voice of revolutionary democracy. There is no coercion in that voice, it is shameful to talk of coercion. Of course, nobody in the ranks of revolutionary democracy would even think of trying to impose power upon a recognised organ created by democracy itself. Even where the demand for a transfer of power took the form of armed demonstrations, this should not be seen as a threat, but merely as a show of force, which the armed people will use in support of the coming "fully popular power".

After all, who could be threatened by this armed force? Does the people have enemies impudent enough to try to silence the people's voice by force of arms? Would not anybody who took up arms here, on the streets of the city, be denounced by the whole people for fratricide? There was no need to carry weapons. They are not needed. We should make this point on the streets, in the barracks and in the factories. We should insist that the flash of cold steel has not distorted the real meaning of the popular demonstrations. But, where this call has not yet reached the ears of the people, we should not take fright or threaten to abandon the revolution. For, we repeat, even where arms have been taken up, they have been taken up not for offensive, but for defensive purposes, not to amplify the people's voice, but to protect it from infringements of its freedom.

It should ring out loud and clear. For it really is time to be done with half-hearted decisions, with the futile attempt, serving only to dissipate the revolution's forces, to reconcile in a single "new order" two irreconcilably hostile worlds, the old world of capitalists and petty bourgeois and the radiant kingdom of labour - the new world, which our revolution has begun to build.

Our revolutionary politics should be an integral whole. For this to happen, our revolutionary power must also be integral, from top to bottom. But this integrity can only be achieved by transferring all power to the only competent organs of revolutionary democracy - the Soviets.

This demand must be fulfilled. We call on our comrade workers and soldiers to refrain from armed demonstrations, from any disorganised actions which serve to reduce the people's strength and right. The transfer of all power to the people without limitations, without deals with the petty bourgeois of the old world, is demanded by life itself, by the revolution itself, and it will come... so long as carelessness, distractions and excessively hot-headed outbursts do not disorganise and disperse the revolutionary forces. We call upon our comrade workers and soldiers to organise, to close ranks, and to express their will calmly and peacefully, in full consciousness of their uncrushable strength.

There have already been attempts at fomenting disorganisation and at goading the masses into violence. Comrades, do not give in to them, because that is the only way your upsurge can be defeated.

Be calm and organise yourselves, comrades!

Long live the unity of the revolutionary people!

Long live revolutionary socialism!

All power to the Soviets of Workers', Soldiers and Peasants' Deputies.

The Organising Committee of Socialist-Revolutionary-Internationalists.
The Socialist-Revolutionary-Internationalist faction of the All-Russian Central Executive Committee of Soviets of Workers' and Soldiers' Deputies.

Source: GARF f. 1834, op. 3, d. 820.
Published in Ya V Leont'ev (compiler), *Partiya levykh sotsialistov-revolyutsionerov, dokumenty i materialy, t. 1, Iyul' 1917 g.-may 1918 g.*, ROSSPEN, Moscow, 2000. pp. 49 - 51.

On 5 July, troops loyal to the government and the Soviet majority were able to quell the disturbances, and the demonstrations dissipated. In the short term, the July episode was very damaging to the far left, in particular the Bolshevik party. The Minister of Justice, the Trudovik P N Pereverzev, produced some documents which purported to show that Lenin was a German agent. Lenin and Zinoviev fled into hiding in Finland, Trotsky spent six weeks in prison. But the right socialists in the government, Mensheviks, SRs and others, were unable to make use of their temporary advantage. They clung doggedly to the notion of a coalition government with non-socialists, even as non-socialists of any calibre willing to serve in the government became harder and harder to find. Kerensky took over as Prime Minister on 8 July, and that same day issued a declaration intended to have broad appeal. It promised to continue the war, but work harder for peace, organise elections to the Constituent Assembly in September, abolish civil inequality, plan the economy, and draft proposals to give the land to the toilers. Kerensky thereby planted his banner firmly in the centre ground of Russian politics – a centre which was eroding rapidly as the economic and military situation deteriorated.

IX. Left and Right Critiques

As the reactions to the July crisis showed once again, the differences between left and right within narodism, just like those within Marxism, reflected fundamental differences in the conception and assessment of the revolution itself. For the right, the revolution was won in February, when the Tsar abdicated, political freedom and equal political rights for all were secured, and a government committed to holding elections to a Constituent Assembly was in place. It was taken as read that the assembly would institute a land reform, and write a constitution for Russia as a parliamentary republic. The Soviets were seen as temporary guarantors of the revolution, and as class institutions of the working people, but certainly not as potential state bodies. Indeed, once a fully-functional parliamentary republic had been established, it is difficult to see any role for the Soviets in the right's conception. For the right, the all-important task was to secure Russian freedom against its external and internal enemies until the Constituent Assembly put the seal on the gains of the revolution. They therefore deprecated anything that weakened the front against Germany, or which contributed further to the disintegration of the Russian state or economy, such as sharp class or national struggles.

The left, as the preceding document eloquently showed, regarded February as just the beginning of a revolution that would lead to socialism, a social order which some imagined in the most florid terms. Their greatest fear was that the revolution would run out of steam, leaving a Russia, maybe with democratic, modernised institutions, but no more equal or fair than any of the other capitalist countries of Europe.

Grigoriy Rivkin, for the SR-Maximalists, saw a class element in the left-right divide, in that the right-wing represented the intelligentsia. At the peasant congress back in May 1917, he had made some rather perceptive remarks about Russia's socialist intellectuals:

Document 24. G A Rivkin on the Revolutionary Intelligentsia

May 1917

The autocracy, which stifled everything that was bright and free in our country, pushed educated people into the ranks of the discontented. The courage of youth made revolutionaries of them, and honest thought made them socialists.

We are talking about the best of them, the sincere ones.

People from gentry, merchant and urban middle class backgrounds, pointlessly persecuted for their convictions, their beliefs, or their nationality, detached themselves from their native milieu and brought their discontent, their knowledge, their urge to be free to the people. They came out as individual fighters against the people's oppressors. The revolution brought those who remained back from hard labour, from exile, and from the underground. They became the people's leaders, in both ideological and practical terms.

The goal of the great majority of the revolutionary intelligentsia is socialism, the complete liberation of the workers, the reign of justice on Earth. But on the road to socialism there are well-lit backstreets and dark ones, crossroads, and junctions. There is the vast enchanted meadow of political freedoms. For poverty-stricken workers and peasants it is full of weeds, thistles and nettles. But for the revolutionary intelligentsia, worn down by prison and persecution, it is a verdant garden. They can speak and write freely in their native language, they can become respected public figures. They can dispute openly with their opponents from other factions, they can pass resolutions and propose their own, they can struggle in dumas, parliaments and even ministries for the proletariat, for the working people. What a prospect! What a temptation! And look! The anarchist, the syndicalist, the revolutionary socialist has become a Trudovik, a People's Socialist, a Kadet! "Let's first consolidate our position, then we can educate the people." And they start to lag behind.

Popular discontent brings forth people who are more revolutionary, who develop more extreme programmes. Now they are in power.

But life is complicated, and their responsibilities are great.

Nor do they have a direct feel for real life, because the people's milieu is not their milieu, the feelings of the people are not their feelings. Their habits and needs are the habits and needs of the educated, the property-owners. From the dizzy heights of power they reach out to the property-owners, to the educated, seeking support. And there they all are, the flatterers and the seducers. "You are great, you are a leader, you are the people's saviour! But look, you're helpless without us, you don't know what to do, but we're with you." And then: "Stop, don't move! There's a bottomless pit ahead..." And these ones start to lag behind, too. And now there remains just a bunch of intellectuals, still true to the social revolution. What saved them from temptation? Are they not of this world, fanatics? Are they deranged fantasists? Or are they firm of character and strong of will? They are all three.

But revolution is war, and requires cool, practical heads, strategists. People who are not of this world, fanatics, prepared for martyrdom, will lead the people to martyrdom as well. They have gone, and still go, towards suffering. Now they are the leaders, and the people are behind them. They bear their cross to Calvary. Deranged fantasists can lead people to struggle and die, but they cannot lead them to victory, because the enemy is intelligent and cunning, laying traps at every step... Only a few people, maybe, are capable of finding the real road.

The main revolutionary intelligentsia detached itself from its roots during the period of underground work. The rest of the working intelligentsia: the teachers, writers, doctors, white-collar workers, and the lawyers, are moderate strata, either in their support for the old order, or in their support for moving forwards, just as they are in the West.

At a time of revolution a part of the working intelligentsia joins the movement for various reasons and merges with the revolutionary intelligentsia, but at first occupies a subordinate position. The revolutionary leadership, the central positions in parties and society, are taken by people from the underground. Living conditions within the working intelligentsia can vary enormously. But, apart from those who own capital, property, factories and shops, and those who get a share of the bosses' haul for special services rendered, they have an interest in establishing the reign of labour on Earth. However, political freedoms on their own also promise them great advantages until such time as our boundless, semi-literate country starts to overproduce intellectuals. For this reason, the practical intellectuals who join with the revolution tend towards the moderate socialist parties. Their great ideals are to be realised some time in the distant future, while for the moment they put forward programmes which give the working intelligentsia every chance to flourish.

Source: Rivkin (Nik. Iv.), *Po puti k Trudovoy Respublike i sotsializmu*, Petrograd, 1917. Published in D B Pavlov, compiler, *Soyuz Eserov-Maksimalistov: dokumenty, publitsistika, 1906 - 1924 gg.*, ROSSPEN, Moscow, 2002, pp. 98 - 99.

A prime example of a politically-moderate revolutionary intellectual, although not one from a privileged background, was Pitirim Sorokin, who had been an SR since his schooldays. In 1917 he worked as Kerensky's secretary, and, as one of the most articulate representatives of the right wing of the SR party, wrote a regular column in the right's paper *Volya naroda* under the rubric "Notes of a sociologist". His writings became increasingly gloomy in the course of 1917, as the right's utopia of a stable, democratic, parliamentary, Westernised Russia looked less and less likely. This piece, from the autumn of 1917, shortly before the Bolsheviks took power, reflects the right-wing socialists' disillusionment with the course of the revolution. At the same time, many of Sorokin's caustic observations about the messianic illusions of the Russian left at that time have more than a ring of truth to them.

Document 25. Pitirim Sorokin: Notes of a sociologist. "Inside-out Slavophilism"

September 1917

Dostoevsky once said: "If you gave a map of the heavens to a Russian schoolboy who knew nothing about astronomy, he would bring it back to you the next day with his own corrections".

This is characteristic of us Russians, and has manifested itself most sharply in Slavophilism, an entire philosophy which elevated Russia to the role of saviour, and asserted its superiority over Western peoples.

"Russia will subjugate the whole world", exclaimed Koshelev.

"We will take a sixth of the world from Europe... the germ of mankind's future development. Russia can become an agency of Providence", wrote Shevyrev, counterposing Russia to the "rotten West".

"My country is destined to provide the world with the long-awaited fruits of Universal enlightenment and sanctify Western inquisitiveness with Eastern faith", wrote Pogodin with equal self-assurance.

The same idea was expressed even more sharply by Kraevsky, Kireevsky, Odoevsky, Aksakov and other Slavophiles. "The God-bearing people", declared Aksakov succinctly. "The power of those forces allotted to us by Providence is so great that it suffices not only for our own perfection, but also to infuse a whole world of new ideas into humanity, to cure the West and save it. Russia will conquer Europe," wrote Odoevsky, "but it will do so spiritually, because only the Russian mind can unite the chaos of European scholarship, shake off the dust of all its authorities and transcend it".

All Slavophilism was suffused with the idea that Russia was higher than other nations, that it had practically nothing to learn from the West while the West had plenty to learn from us, that the West was rotting and that the task of our country was to save both the West and all humanity by coming to their aid.

All this was said with conviction and sincerity. The "Russian schoolboy", in the guise of the Slavophiles, having only just learned something from the West, was already dismissing it, and elevating poor, unenlightened, enserfed Russia to the role of teacher and saviour of the "rotten and confused" West.

This picture deserves our attention. We should recall it now, because Slavophilism in various guises lives on. It is particularly fashionable these days.

I am referring first and foremost to present-day Bolshevism, and, indirectly, to a significant part of our revolutionary democracy.

Bolshevism is surely that same Slavophilism inside out. Look at its ideology, pay attention to its phraseology, to the articles, plans and speeches of the Bolsheviks, and you will surely be struck by its complete similarity to the main lines of Slavophilism. "The Russian revolutionary democracy is the vanguard of world socialism." "We are the pioneers of the revolution." "We must come to the aid of the Western European proletariat in its struggle with imperialism. We must help it." "We have shown how to fight for peace and wage the class struggle. Let our Western comrades learn from us." "We must save the world from war and we will do so." "Let the Western proletariat know that it can count on our experience, knowledge, will and complete support for its struggle."

Such proud phrases as these are common in Bolshevik speeches. A large part of our revolutionary democracy is also guilty of using them.

Drunk with success, we really imagine ourselves to be the "vanguard and advance party of world socialism". Just like the Slavophiles, we have come to believe that we are indeed the saviours of humanity, that the Western proletariat can count on our bounteous support, that we are graciously prepared to instruct it and will not refuse to take on the great mission of saving humanity from war and all the evils of imperialism.

Having come to believe all this, we have proudly addressed appeals "to the peoples of the world", and sent our Argonauts to the West to seek out and achieve world peace. Moreover, according to Lenin, Russia has already outgrown the form of the democratic republic. In his opinion it can now lay claim to something more - to a government of the Paris Commune type. The West has not yet reached the stage of a socialist majority government, while we are already demanding a proletarian dictatorship. The "bourgeoisified" West has never thought of concluding peace in secret, but we have. The West's bourgeoisified democracy has not dared proclaim and immediately wage a "merciless war until victory over capital", but our Bolsheviks have. On a daily basis, with the all daring of a "leading vanguard", they trumpet a merciless war of peasants against landowners, of workers against capitalists, and of the revolutionary democracy against world imperialism.

The imperialist West is in no shape to restore the International. We shall boldly undertake that task.

What is all this, other than inside-out Slavophilism? Isn't this the same self-importance that the Slavophiles had? Isn't this the same sort of Providential role for Russia that the Slavophiles claimed? And who is saying all this? Marxists, Bolsheviks, who always used to reproach the Narodniks with Slavophile sympathies and demand that Russia be recast in industrial furnaces.

Petty, talentless people, who have contributed nothing to humanity, don the mantles of the world's saviours. Errant Russian intellectuals - the Lunacharskies and the Trotskies, the Lenins and the Zinovievs, or worse still, the likes of Posse, who has been hopelessly confused by the simplest things all his life - act as if they were Spartacus, the world's chosen and anointed leaders. The Russian proletariat, ignorant, up to 80% illiterate with the rest barely able to read and write, is so mesmerised by revolutionary phraseology that it is seriously beginning to believe that it is the "leading, most conscious and best detachment of the International". When you look at all this, you cannot help thinking of the Slavophiles and Dostoevsky's "Russian schoolboy"...

When you hear these speeches at meetings and in the papers even now, when the revolution is in its death throes, when Russia is dying from its ignorance, savagery, inability to live and create, when life is raining blow after blow upon us, revealing all our backwardness, you cannot help feeling exasperated. You also feel embarrassed for our revolutionary democracy and its "leaders" in front of our Western colleagues and comrades.

In the past the pretensions of the Slavophiles were ridiculed by a whole series of people, especially Chaadaev. What can the Western socialist leaders and the Western proletariat be saying about us now?

They would be quite justified in quoting the words of the great Chaadaev back at us: "Only we Russians have given nothing to the world, we have not contributed one idea to the mass of human thought, we have not assisted the progress of human reason and have distorted everything that we have acquired from that progress... We Russians do not have enough consistency in our thinking and have not mastered Western syllogism... We grow, but we do not mature, we move forward, but along a crooked line which does not lead to our goal, we are like children who have not been taught to think properly." Our Western comrades would be quite justified, like Chaadaev, in saying of us now: "We Russians do not belong to one of the great families of the human race, we belong neither to the West nor to the East. We have neither the traditions of one, nor of the other, nor have we been touched by humanity's global enlightenment". Could they not also characterise our revolution in the same way that the great Westerniser described our history: barbarism, crude ignorance and a violent and degraded dominion of distorted and poorly understood Western ideas?

They won't say it out loud, because they are too polite. But their diplomatic and courteous refusal to go to the Stockholm conference once the helplessness and disorganisation of our "leading vanguard" became apparent must surely be their tacit, but highly eloquent, verdict on us.

Source: *Volya naroda* No. 116, September 1917
Published on: www.yabloko.ru/Themes/History/Sorokin/sorokin-2.html

Pitirim Aleksandrovich Sorokin

X. Late summer and autumn 1917: the SRs in crisis

As the military, economic and social crisis in Russia worsened, support for the government, for the leading SR-Menshevik bloc in the Soviet Executive Committee, and for the SR party itself ebbed away, especially in the cities. In mid-July, Kerensky had appointed General Lavr Kornilov – known as an advocate of stronger military discipline and the renewed use of capital punishment in the army – as Commander-in-Chief. At the end of August, Kornilov moved troops towards Petrograd, ostensibly to thwart a planned Bolshevik coup. Whether Kornilov actually intended to seize power himself is unclear, but Kerensky, after initial hesitation, declared Kornilov's actions to be a revolt against the government and dismissed him as C-in-C on 27 August. Kerensky had to appeal to the Soviets to organise workers' militias and revolutionary sailors to defend Petrograd. In the event, Kornilov's forces never reached Petrograd – Soviet and other delegations met them en route and dissuaded them from continuing, and the supposed coup attempt fizzled out. But for a few days the atmosphere in Petrograd was extremely tense. The entire Soviet spectrum – from the most moderate SRs right through to the anarchists – mobilised to defend the revolution against the forces of reaction. Senior Naval Lieutenant Vasiliy Filippovsky, a leading local SR, played a prominent role in the Petrograd Soviet's mobilisation against Kornilov. He reported on the measures taken to a private session of the Soviet on 29 August.

Document 26. *Golos soldata*'s account of V N Filippovsky's report to the Petrograd Soviet on the Kornilov revolt.

29 August 1917

The session opened at 7:45 p.m. with a report from Comrade Filippovsky on the current military situation. The speaker outlined all the measures taken by the organisations set up to combat the counterrevolutionary conspiracy, in particularly the Provisional Military Committee. The speaker remarked with satisfaction that, at last, a united revolutionary front has been created in the ranks of the revolutionary democracy. The speaker then stated that the counterrevolution had only infected the top military command, the masses of soldiers had not been affected by it at all. Those units who moved on Petrograd had been influenced by the foulest provocation from their commanding officers. It had been difficult at first to inform the army of its mistake, because the commanders had taken over the telephones and telegraph beforehand. However, links with the army had now been established, and messages were coming in from everywhere expressing their loyalty to the Provisional Government. The speaker then acquainted the meeting with the measures that had been taken by the military district command, along with the Provisional Military Committee, to defend Petrograd, and with the fact that a special organisation had been formed to work out a plan to arm the working masses of Petrograd.

In response to questions, Comrade Filippovsky announced the arrest of officers in the Astoria Hotel, including the chairman of the Military League, General Fedorov, whose premises were searched and documents confiscated.

Source: *Golos soldata*, No. 101, 30 August 1917, p. 4.
Published in N Yu Cherepenina et al. (compilers), *Petrogradskiy sovet rabochikh i soldatskikh deputatov v 1917 godu*, Vol. 4. ROSSPEN, Moscow, 2003, p. 233.

However, many of those mobilised to defend the revolution were in no mood to defend the Provisional Government and its policies, especially as Kerensky was soon widely believed to have encouraged Kornilov to act in the first place. The Kornilov revolt greatly boosted support for the left, and the Bolsheviks were the main beneficiaries. The chaos in the armed forces deepened still further.

In the aftermath of the Kornilov revolt, Chernov finally resigned his position as agriculture minister. Having previously acquiesced in government policies with barely a murmur of protest, Chernov now launched a broadside against the government. As a wave of peasant disturbances and land seizures swept the country, he laid the blame squarely at the door of his former cabinet colleagues.

Document 27. V Chernov. From an article: "The Only Way Out"

30 September 1917

We are sorry to say it, but we were expecting this. We were expecting something predicted by everyone who has dealings with the countryside and understands it. We were expecting the outbreak of mass agrarian disturbances.

There was only one way these disturbances could have been averted. There should have been revolutionary legislation to embrace all aspects of our national life. A firm legal basis for the operation of the local land committees should have been created. We should have been ahead of events, not lagging behind them. From the very beginning of the revolution, new temporary laws should have been quickly enacted to regulate all land use and all the agrarian relationships between different groups of the population. The land committees should have been made into stable, authoritative local state organs, able to take timely measures – powerfully and decisively where necessary – to avert outbursts. They should have been able to make concessions to reasonable demands, where the people's needs were not being met.

But instead we delayed, delayed, and delayed again. Absolutely every measure aimed at interfering with the old unfettered prerogatives of landowners met with fierce opposition both inside and outside the coalition government. Some proposed legislation, concerned, for example, with the hay harvest, with accounting for and organising the supply of hay to the army and the towns, with measures to assist harvesting, was either deferred or put through endless procedures, until the hay gathering or the harvesting were already over and the proposals had to be dropped. With other measures it was like getting a rope through the eye of a needle. They had to get through the purgatory of the Legal Convention, and then get past the Provisional Government. When at last they were published, they had been mangled, and were late to boot. Yet other measures are still waiting to be enacted. It was as if everybody was quietly confident that there was no hurry. It was as if nobody understood that there can be perilous times, when even an imperfect law brought out in good time is better than a more perfect law that is too late to calm people whose patience is exhausted. It was as if it were possible to *sit out* an agrarian question, which the war and revolution had made much more acute, until the convocation of the continually-delayed Constituent Assembly...

...The trouble is that the agrarian riots that have begun provide wide opportunities for the dregs of society, exacerbating their mindlessly destructive side still further. The trouble is that they may spread from one place to another in a mass psychotic epidemic, growing into an avalanche.

There is no time to lose. Once the fire has started, you cannot put it out. We need immediate heroic measures to stop this movement while it is still localised. How to do it? With the tried and trusted method of the punitive expedition? The occasional paroxysms of "firm authority" that sometimes seize our politicians might suggest that method. But I would ask: who can be sure that a policy of naked repression would not be ineffectual? Who can be sure that those same peasants in soldiers' greatcoats would obediently obey their orders to pacify the countryside? Who is unaware that the Cossacks sent to put down agrarian disorders feel themselves between the devil and the deep blue sea – an agitated peasantry and agitated garrisons in the rear? They often grumble that once again, just like in the old days, they are being used in ways that just generate hostility to them as professional repressors. And finally, who cannot understand the risks the government would be running when the news of punitive expeditions in the villages, embellished by rumour, reached the front – a front which has only just regained its equilibrium?

...There is only one way out. ...the way to avert agrarian disorders is to *put the land under the control of the land committees.*

Source: *Delo naroda*, No. 168, 30 September 1917.
Published in N D Erofeev, compiler, *Partiya sotisialistov-revolyutsionerov. Dokumenty i materialy*, Vol. 3 part 1, ROSSPEN, Moscow, 2000, pp. 821 – 825.

This outbreak of agrarian disorders showed that the peasants' patience, and their willingness to follow the SR leadership, were wearing thin. The Left SRs, who supported this radical mood among the peasants, were the main political beneficiaries of the shift in peasant attitudes. SR support among urban workers and soldiers was plummeting even faster. At the Moscow City Duma elections on 25 June, the SRs had gained almost 60% of the votes cast, while the Bolsheviks won around 12%. Three months later, at the elections for the Moscow district councils on 24 September, these proportions had been reversed – on a lower poll, the Bolsheviks won 51% and the SRs just 14%. Support for the Kadets on the right had also risen. Writing in *Delo naroda*, the veteran narodnik Osip Minor put a brave face on these results, laying the whole blame for his party's rout on the illusions and fickleness of the "unenlightened masses" – whose support the SRs had been only too glad to receive in June. But he also noted something even more ominous for the SRs than a defeat at the polls: a more general disillusionment in the ability of "democracy" to create a better life in Russia.

Document 28. O S Minor: *Letters from Moscow*

30 September 1917

On the 24th I took the last train from tense, smouldering Petrograd to tranquil Moscow.

In my carriage the usual conversations were taking place. At first, my neighbours, an engineer and a lawyer, were cursing the Provisional Government and Kerensky in particular, who, "as everyone knows", knew that Kornilov was not a traitor but was "carrying out" Kerensky's own orders. Then they were cursing "bureaucratic Petrograd" for the fact that red tape in the departments was causing chaos much worse than under Nicholas, and finally they were outraged by the price rises, that the government was doing nothing to combat.

In a word, "democracy has not improved" the situation, it has even made things worse compared to how they were before the revolution. "Democracy has destroyed the army!", "Democracy has created these useless Soviets!", "The Soviets are destabilising the government!", and on, and on and on.

Democracy is now getting the blame for all the ills previously laid at the door of Tsarism. It is as if people are being psychologically prepared to overthrow democracy in favour of something better able to improve the material situation in the country. The methods of agitation against democracy are strikingly similar to the ones used against the autocracy.

And indeed, the revolution has not removed the defects of the autocratic system in our daily lives. The general chaos means that people have to put up with more from these defects than they did before the revolution. Is it at all surprising that discontent is mounting?

"Fixed prices caused the revolution," says one of my companions.

"The same fixed prices for grain will cause another one," says the other, "the same causes will bring about the same effects. Fixed prices caused the fall of Tsarism, they will kill the revolution as well".

Thus the night passed. I listened, without getting involved in the conversation, and it was very painful to realise that there was a lot of truth in it all.

I pictured the chaos in the ranks of the democracy itself; I recalled the way the Bolsheviks agitate against the other socialist parties, with all that shouting about the Democratic Conference betraying the cause of the proletariat, the struggle of the working people. I thought that in Moscow, people would not be so blunt and rude about each other.

Alas, my illusions were far removed from reality.

The struggle against democracy in our country is being fought on two fronts, and the results of the district duma elections showed that very clearly. The Bolsheviks and the Kadets gained their successes by one and the same methods, by agitation against the centre, against the Socialist-Revolutionaries. By the side of the ballot boxes, the Bolsheviks were denouncing the Socialist-Revolutionaries: "They promised you loads, but have done nothing; they have put up the tram fares! They don't care, they all went to university, they are earning thousands, they don't mind paying more, they don't care about the working people at all!" And the Kadets were singing the refrain: "We are for freedom, we are for order, which the socialists have not given you and cannot give you!"

On the basis of such irresponsible criticism success among the unenlightened masses is assured, and it was the Bolsheviks and Kadets who were victorious in the district dumas. Our lists only garnered the votes of our conscious supporters. And in this we can see a good omen for our party.

As we saw at an earlier stage, our success in the elections to the central Moscow Duma was the result of exaggerated hopes on the part of the unenlightened masses that the Socialist-Revolutionaries would be able to eliminate inflation, increase wages by 50 – 100%, abolish the housing shortage and the queues at baker's and shoe shops, etc. It was clear to us that we would not be able to justify those expectations, that dealing with these phenomena would require persistent work over a long time, especially since the chaos in Moscow was closely connected with the chaos across the country, which was growing and deepening all the time.

But for the Bolsheviks of left and right, this gave them a basis for agitating against us and ensuring their success at the district elections. On the face of it, we suffered a defeat, but it allowed us to see what are our real party forces, those forces who will not desert us. Our defeat among the unenlightened masses has cleansed the ranks of our party of that slime which now adorns the Kadets and the Bolsheviks.

It can be said with certainty that neither one nor the other will be able to do any more than the objective circumstances permit. Within 2 – 3 weeks they will start to get all the accusations that have been levelled against the Moscow Duma, because they are even less able than the duma to provide the city with bread, shoes, meat etc. The disintegration of economic life has progressed so far that the only way to survive it is by the whole population working in a determined and planned fashion.

It is therefore obvious that domestic policies of divide and rule are especially dangerous here.

The Bolsheviks' victory, which has been gained on just that basis, is a Pyrrhic victory, and we are sure they will soon realise this very clearly.

For us Socialist-Revolutionaries, this is only a superficial defeat. It will serve to cleanse the party of "perishable products", of politically promiscuous people who, like flies, are attracted to light sources of any type.

Our party is now gathering the genuinely party elements behind its banners. It is re-forming its ranks, and will march boldly along the path it marked out long ago, sweeping aside all the demagogic filth from the sewers.

Source: *Delo naroda*, No. 168, 30 September 1917.
Published in N D Erofeev, compiler, *Partiya sotisialistov-revolyutsionerov. Dokumenty i materialy*, Vol. 3 part 1, ROSSPEN, Moscow, 2000, pp. 807 - 808.

Alas for Osip Minor and his comrades, not only were the SRs' ranks dwindling, they were increasingly out of step with one another. Nor was there much consensus as to which path they should be marching along. The key issue, by the autumn of 1917, was the question of "Soviet power". It was not an issue with much scope for compromise.

Viktor Mikhaylovich Chernov

XI. Soviet Power

From the outset, the Soviets were powerful organisations – indeed, much of the Provisional Government's legitimacy rested on its recognition by the Soviets. But there was never any agreement in the Soviet camp about *how much* power the Soviets ought to wield, and *how* it should be exercised. The original conception of the right-wing SR-Menshevik bloc was not to take a direct part in government at all, but once Soviet representatives had formally joined the government in May 1917, this bloc clung tenaciously to the idea of a coalition with the propertied elements, mainly represented by the Kadets. The SR left criticised this policy of coalition, and called instead for a government answerable to the Soviets, comprised solely of representatives of Soviet parties. Isaak Shteynberg gave a typical formulation of this line in an (unsuccessful) motion he put at the 7th council meeting of the SR party in early August 1917.

Document 29. From I Z Shteynberg's motion to the 7th PSR council

9 August 1917

...3. Noting the collapse of every attempt to create some kind of coalition government in an ever-sharpening class struggle ... the 7th council of the SR party considers that the basic questions of the Russian revolution can only be solved if a *homogeneous* government is formed, based on the country's revolutionary working classes. Such a government can only be a government of the revolutionary democracy itself, answerable to the Soviet of Workers', Soldiers' and Peasants' Deputies and the democratised organs of local government. ...

Source: *Delo naroda*, No. 124, 12 August 1917.
Published in N D Erofeev, compiler, *Partiya sotisialistov-revolyutsionerov. Dokumenty i materialy*, Vol. 3 part 1, ROSSPEN, Moscow, 2000, pp. 721 - 722.

The formulation "homogenous government" became a standard demand of the left in the SR and Menshevik parties in the autumn of 1917. It referred to a government composed solely of representatives of socialist parties, "from the People's Socialists to the Bolsheviks", as resolutions of the time often put it. Such a government, its advocates imagined, would undertake radical measures to tackle the crisis before the convocation of the Constituent Assembly, but would then cede power to whatever government emerged from the nationwide elections. It should be noted that this demand for a socialist government *answerable* to the Soviets was not the same as Lenin's policy that the Soviets should themselves *become* the government.

By the autumn, when the long-postponed elections to the Constituent Assembly were at last within sight, the SR party leadership had no interest in experimenting with novel forms of government. Despite the party's precipitate loss of support among the urban working class and the soldiers since the summer, they had maintained their position much better in the countryside, despite the growing rural unrest. With Russia's overwhelming peasant majority, the SRs were assured of a strong showing at the polls – if they could only hang on until then. The major threat to this perspective came from the growing clamour for "Soviet power", as the SR-Menshevik blocs lost power to the Bolsheviks in Soviet elections in Petrograd, Moscow, and elsewhere. In this situation, the timing of the forthcoming 2nd All-Russia Congress of Soviets acquired a crucial importance. The SR and Menshevik leaderships were anxious for it to be postponed until after the assembly elections.

Document 30. *Delo naroda* editorial: "The Soviets and the Constituent Assembly"

6 October 1917

The question of the relationship between the Soviets, the authoritative organs of revolutionary democracy, and the Constituent Assembly, the sovereign organ of the people's will and power, has once again been raised in the pages of the socialist press.

The reason for this has been the timing of the convocation of the All-Russia Congress of Soviets of Workers' and Soldiers' Deputies - 20 October. Falling right in the midst of the election campaign, this timing has led to strong objections. These have come not only from the Executive Committee of the All-Russia Soviet of Peasants' Deputies, which considers the calling of the congress for 20 October "untimely and dangerous", but also from army organisations, which have pointed to the complete impossibility of diverting their best forces from preparing for the Constituent Assembly elections.

The revolutionary democracy has to attract tens of millions of men and women, who are only coming to political activity for the first time, to participate consciously in the elections. Given the massive size of our country, its lack of roads and the poverty of its intellectual resources, one would think that the magnitude of this task would, for simple considerations of expediency and political calculation, cause the congress to be postponed until the period between the end of polling and the opening of the Constituent Assembly. Instead, the Bolshevik press, by means of a whole series of exaggerations, slanderous insinuations and distortions of facts, is trying to present the matter as if the postponement of the congress reflects a desire to "get rid" of the Soviets, a "betrayal of the revolution", a "sell out of the working class" and even the "wrecking of the Constituent Assembly". Sick ideas displace healthy ones, as they say.

What is the matter here? And, first of all, a general question: should the Soviets disappear with the opening of the Constituent Assembly; can both institutions coexist at the same time? The Soviets are *class organs of the workers, soldiers and peasants*. When the revolution managed at one stroke to remove Tsarism's entire state organisation, all the machinery of compulsion and authority upon which the old order rested, the Soviets arose in the place of the defunct government machinery. The force of events made them into *revolutionary organs, that is, organs of state power at the centre and in the localities.* In this way, a class organisation of the working people became endowed with state authority.

But this kind of power structure, so unusual in the present period, was brought about exclusively by the disappearance of the old, autocratic state organs. The people were drawn to the Soviets as the only institutions in the country, the provinces, and the villages, that could re-establish broken economic and administrative links and serve as a cement, something on which the people could rely. But as soon as new elements of state organisation were created, town dumas and zemstvos suited to a modern democratic state, this immediately posed the question of the limits of the Soviets' *state* powers. And this question will become even more pressing with the opening of the Constituent Assembly as the only bearer of supreme power.

We consider that under the capitalist economic system in which we are now living and which – until the socialist revolution in Western Europe – will remain the basic economic reality in our country, the republic of Soviets can only be the class organisation of the working people. This can and should carry an enormous weight in the political and economic life of the country, but is not the basic component element of the state organisation of a democratic republic. The only thing that is incompatible with the opening of a Constituent Assembly, elected on the basis of universal, direct and equal suffrage is the struggle to overthrow it under the slogan of "all power to the Soviets". But powerful organisations of workers and peasants are not only compatible, but essential in the course of the Constituent Assembly's work. Only with their help will it be possible to put the decisions of the Constituent Assembly into effect, and only their presence in the country can provide a firm guarantee of the democratic nature and justice of these decisions.

Therefore, the Bolsheviks' slanderous campaign against those peasants' and soldiers' organisations and socialist parties which have come out in favour of postponing the congress of Soviets until the period between the end of the polls for the Constituent Assembly and the opening of the Assembly, is motivated simply by an unwillingness to accept the impending collapse of Bolshevism's main tactical slogan of transferring state power to the Soviets. And, in objecting to holding the congress of Soviets on 20 October and proposing another date, such as 20 November, we are not attempting to render the revolutionary organs of democracy ineffectual. On the contrary, we want to link them with the socialist representation in the Constituent Assembly, so that the socialist parties, based on the authoritative organs of revolutionary democracy, will be able boldly and decisively to implement their election platforms and promises.

Source: *Delo naroda*, No. 173, 6 October 1917.
Published in N D Erofeev, compiler, *Partiya sotisialistov-revolyutsionerov. Dokumenty i materialy*, Vol. 3 part 1, ROSSPEN, Moscow, 2000, pp. 825-827.

In the event, the Congress of Soviets was called for 25 October. By the time it opened, the Petrograd Soviet's Military-Revolutionary Committee, acting under Bolshevik direction, had taken control of various locations around Petrograd and declared the Provisional Government to be overthrown. As the Bolsheviks had around 250 of the 513 delegates to the congress, and leftists constituted a considerable part of the SR delegation, it was clear that the congress would approve this action and declare the establishment of Soviet power.

The SR delegation met before the opening of the congress. Predictably enough, it was fundamentally divided on how to assess the overturn and the tactics to adopt. Some of the delegates had been directly involved in deposing the government, while the official line of their own party was to abandon the congress in protest. The following report, from the newspaper *Znamya truda*, which supported the left, shows the range of positions.

Document 31. Meeting of the Socialist-Revolutionary faction at the All-Russia Congress of Soviets

25 October 1917

The session opens at 12.00 noon, chaired by **S Mstislavsky**. Around 200 delegates to the All-Russia Congress are present, along with many members of the Socialist-Revolutionary faction of the Petrograd Soviet, members of the Petrograd Committee of the SR Party, members of the regional committee and representatives of the Central Committee.

One comrade, a member of the Military-Revolutionary Committee, gives a report on the activities of the MRC. Having heard the report, the faction moves on to discuss the latest events. The questions are: 1) the attitude to the overthrow of the government, and 2) the attitude to power. An enormous number apply to speak.

Comrade **L'vov** calls for a homogeneous socialist government drawn from the All-Russia Soviet.

Comrade **Nesterov** insists that the All-Russia Congress, supplemented by peasant deputies, should continue the cause of the Petrograd Soviet of Workers' and Soldiers' Deputies.

Comrade **Filippovsky** calls for a general democratic government.

Comrade **Gendel'man** speaks on behalf of the Socialist-Revolutionary Party CC. He calls above all for party unity, and says that the only difference between the party centre and the left wing concerns the possibility of forming a homogeneous government. Coming out sharply against the Bolsheviks, Gendel'man says that a homogenous revolutionary government would be under Bolshevik hegemony, and the Bolsheviks themselves are in thrall to the elemental course of events. The [SR] party must not let itself be used by anybody, and for that reason the complete isolation of the Bolsheviks is vital. There must not be any contact with them. Comrades Kamkov, Karelin, Malkin and Kolegaev respond to the CC representative.

Comrade **Kamkov** says that it is impossible to walk away from living events. Isolating the Bolsheviks would be equivalent to abandoning life, isolating oneself from world events that are taking place. The SR party would retire to the back yard of history.

Comrade **Karelin** supports Kamkov and says that Lenin, who advocates communism – a federation of individual independent communes – is not the sum total of Bolshevism. The Bolsheviks are a necessary element. If this cause fails, it is not only the Bolsheviks who will fail.

Comrade **Malkin**, speaking along the same lines, insists on the most active participation in what is happening and says that "you can do deals with the Kadets, but you can't do deals with history".

A proposal is made to elect a commission to find out the basis on which the Bolsheviks intend to form a government.

Comrade **Gots** objects strongly – no contacts – and reads out the CC resolution on the withdrawal of all members of the Socialist-Revolutionary Party from the All-Russia Soviet Congress and all organisations where the Bolsheviks are working.

The proposal to elect a commission to make contact with the Bolsheviks is adopted by a majority. Kamkov and Karelin are elected onto the commission, and a place is offered to the CC, which delegates Firsov. The discussions continue.

A representative of the united faction of Social-Democratic Menshevik-Internationalists is given the floor at our congress to make an extraordinary statement. He reads out a resolution adopted by their faction. The resolution considers that a united front of the revolutionary democracy is vital. It remarks that the isolation of the Bolshevik comrades would mean the defeat of the revolution, and therefore the Menshevik-Internationalists have resolved to take part in building a new revolutionary government, and call on the Socialist-Revolutionaries to do likewise.

Comrade **Filippovsky** reads out a resolution of the railway trade union which states that the union places itself at the disposal of the [Soviet] Central Executive Committee and the new one to be elected by the congress.

After a break the question of whether to walk out of the All-Russia Congress or to take part in its work is put to the vote. For the walkout – 63, for participation – 92, abstentions – 9. Once the results are announced, the centre group, finding itself in a minority, announces that it is forming a separate faction and leaves the meeting.

Source: A S Pokrovsky, E Yu Tikhonova, compilers, *Vtoroy vserossiyskiy s"ezd sovetov rabochikh i soldatskikh deputatov (25-26 oktyabrya 1917 g.)*, Arkheograficheskiy tsentr, Moscow, 1997, pp. 117 – 118.

At the congress itself, Mikhail Gendel'man, representing the PSR CC, denounced the overturn. In protest at the bombardment of the Winter Palace, where ministers from his party were under siege, he led part of the SR delegation – the part that still followed the party leadership – out of the congress. Needless to say, this walkout suited the Bolsheviks admirably.

Document 32. Declaration by M Ya Gendel'man, for the Socialist-Revolutionary Party, at the opening session of the 2nd All-Russia Congress of Soviets

25 October 1917

The Socialist-Revolutionary faction of the All-Russia Congress of Workers' and Soldiers' Deputies, in accordance with the CC of the Socialist-Revolutionary Party declares: 1. The seizure of power carried out by the Bolshevik Party and the Petrograd Soviet of Workers' and Soldiers' Deputies, on the eve of the Constituent Assembly and one day before the opening of the All-Russia Congress of Workers' and Soldiers' Deputies, is a crime against the motherland and the revolution. It marks the beginning of civil war, the destruction of the Constituent Assembly and threatens the end of the revolution. 2. The Bolsheviks' promises are obviously unrealisable in the present conditions. Once this becomes apparent, there will inevitably be an explosion of popular indignation. Anticipating this, the Socialist-Revolutionary faction calls on all the revolutionary forces in the country to get organised and defend the revolution, taking the fate of the country into their own hands. In this way they can prevent the counterrevolution from triumphing in the coming catastrophe, and ensure the speediest conclusion of a general democratic peace, the convocation of the Constituent Assembly at the designated time and the socialisation of the land. 3. Power has been seized by the Bolsheviks and the Petrograd Soviet of Workers' and Soldiers' Deputies, which they control. The Socialist-Revolutionary faction holds them fully responsible for all the consequences of their insane and criminal act, and, given that it is impossible to work with them, leaves the congress.

Source: A S Pokrovsky, E Yu Tikhonova, compilers, *Vtoroy vserossiyskiy s''ezd sovetov rabochikh i soldatskikh deputatov (25-26 oktyabrya 1917 g.)*, Arkheograficheskiy tsentr, Moscow, 1997, pp. 99 – 100.

The immediate public denunciation of the Bolshevik overturn issued by the SR Central Committee was uncompromising, shrill, and, in places, quite prophetic:

Document 33. Appeal of the Socialist-Revolutionary Party Central Committee "To Workers, Peasants, Soldiers and Sailors"

26 October 1917

"In struggle you will find your rights."

Comrade workers, peasants, soldiers and sailors!

You have been basely and criminally deceived!

The seizure of power has been carried out by the Bolsheviks alone. They have abused the name of the Petrograd Soviet of Workers' and Soldiers' Deputies, because the Bolsheviks were hiding their plans from the other socialist parties in the Soviet.

This seizure of power has been carried out three weeks before the convocation of the Constituent Assembly, and one day before the opening of the All-Russia Congress of Soviets of Workers' and Soldiers' Deputies.

When the congress opened and recognised the accomplished fact of the seizure of power it was exceeding its own powers, as all the socialist parties and front delegates had walked out, leaving just the Bolsheviks and those socialist-revolutionary-maximalists who hang on to their coat-tails.

The voice of the working peasantry was not heard. The peasant soviets refused to attend the congress, as it was necessary to work in the localities for the elections to the Constituent Assembly. The All-Russia Executive Committee of Soviets of Peasants' Deputies has protested against the insanity of the Bolsheviks. The Bolsheviks apprehended No. 147 of *Izvestiya Vserossiyskogo soveta krest'yanskikh deputatov** and shut the printworks, using gendarme methods to stifle the free voice of the working peasantry.

You have been promised bread, but there will be no bread. The Bolsheviks' rising has completed the chaos on the railways, and even before then we were having trouble ensuring the delivery of grain.

The fact that the Bolsheviks are in power will not cause any new locomotives or wagons to appear or any extra coal to be mined, but the fact that the Bolsheviks have brought about a civil war on the eve of the Constituent Assembly and have destroyed the entire state apparatus will ensure that we will be left completely without either railways or coal.

As a result of the destruction of state power, the banks will be obliged to cease their operations. There will be no money. You will receive neither benefits nor wages.

The Bolsheviks will lead you to the closure of plants and factories, to unemployment and death from starvation.

They have promised you immediate peace, but have given you a new revolution that nobody will deal with – neither our enemies nor our allies. The embassies are leaving. The Bolsheviks have untied the Allies' hands to reach a

* "News of the All-Russia Soviet of Peasants' Deputies"

peace with Germany exclusively at the expense of Russia.

They have promised you immediate peace, but instead will give you a new, most onerous war at the front and a new civil war throughout the country.

They have promised you land and freedom, but the counterrevolution will use the anarchy sown by the Bolsheviks to deprive you of both land and freedom.

In the resolution of the Bolshevik Soviet of Workers' and Soldiers' Deputies announcing the seizure of power there is not a word about the Constituent Assembly.

You were on the eve of the Constituent Assembly – the Bolsheviks have wrecked it.

The only way to put an end to the anarchy and the already exultant counterrevolution is to create a new revolutionary democratic government which will be recognised by the whole country.

Close ranks around the Committee to Save the Motherland and Revolution, around the socialist parties. They will create a new homogeneous revolutionary-democratic government, and this government will immediately pass the land to the land committees, propose a general democratic peace to all the warring countries, put an end to anarchy and counterrevolution and lead the country to the Constituent Assembly.

Comrade workers, peasants, soldiers and sailors!

You have been basely and criminally deceived. Do not listen to the Bolsheviks, throw them out, let this gang of renegades from the revolution remain isolated, and then their rising will come to an end immediately and without any bloodshed.

Central Committee, Party of Socialist-Revolutionaries
26 October 1917

Source: *Delo naroda*, No. 191, 28 October 1917.
Published in N D Erofeev, compiler, *Partiya sotsialistov-revolyutsionerov, Dokumenty i materialy, Oktyabr' 1917 g. - 1925 g. t. 3, ch. 2.* ROSSPEN, Moscow, 2000, pp. 31 – 32.

The Committee to Save the Motherland and Revolution, chaired by Abram Gots, tried immediately to rally the army, local authorities, the socialist parties and so on to resist the Bolsheviks' seizure of power. It led the ill-fated revolt of officer cadets ("Junkers") in Petrograd on 29 October, but overall it failed to find many people willing to risk their lives to restore Kerensky. This very first attempt at armed resistance to Bolshevik rule ended in fiasco. The Bolsheviks clearly enjoyed a considerable degree of support.

In complete contrast to the main SR party, the Left SRs who stayed at the Soviet congress recognised the overthrow of the Provisional Government as legitimate. They were, however, unhappy with the Bolsheviks' *fait accompli* in designating a Council of People's Commissars, and still hoped for a broader left, "homogeneous democratic" government. At the Soviet congress, in the early morning of 26 October, the leading Left SR Vladimir Karelin expressed his group's concerns.

Document 34. V A Karelin's speech at the 2nd All-Russia Congress of Soviets – *Znamya truda*'s résumé

26 October 1917

The Left Socialist Revolutionaries favour uniting the majority of the revolutionary democracy. As an alternative to the principle of coalition, we advance the principle of a homogenous democratic government. We think it is essential to bring about an agreement between the Bolshevik comrades and the other socialist parties. Nobody has taken any steps to unite the socialist parties. We consider the formation of a democratic government to be the only way out of this situation. The Congress of Soviets is the best and most authoritative organ for creating this, but here we have been presented with a fully-formed government. We protest against this also on the grounds that this administration will not have been approved by the Congress of Peasants' Deputies. At this congress there are only a few random representatives from the peasants. We are opposed to the isolation of the Bolsheviks, and we are aware of our duty to the revolution. We could have had our names on that government list, but then we would no longer be able to act as conciliators. To sum up: 1) Inasmuch as it is necessary to organise a government, we will support any attempt to do so. 2) Inasmuch as the Bolshevik comrades are making the transition to a homogeneous democratic government more difficult, we will vote against.

Source: A S Pokrovsky, E Yu Tikhonova, compilers, *Vtoroy vserossiyskiy s''ezd sovetov rabochikh i soldatskikh deputatov (25-26 oktyabrya 1917 g.)*, Arkheograficheskiy tsentr, Moscow, 1997, p. 121.

But conciliation, as the Left SRs envisaged it, was not a realistic option. The Bolsheviks, committed to Soviet power, were disinclined to compromise with parties committed to a parliamentary republic unless compelled to do so. Even the most radical of the other socialist groups only favoured a *temporary* Soviet-based government, to cover the period before the Constituent Assembly met. And the SR leadership, desperate to do something about the debilitating divisions within their party, moved against the left-wing rebels.

Document 35. Resolution of the SR Party CC: "On the expulsion from the party of those members who took part with the Bolsheviks in the October armed uprising and failed to leave the 2nd All-Russia Congress of Soviets of Workers' and Soldiers' Deputies"

27 October 1917

All members of the party who took part in the Bolshevik adventure and did not leave the Congress of Soviets after the bombardment of the Winter Palace, the arrest of party members and other acts of violence committed by the Military-

Revolutionary Committee against the democracy are excluded from the party for gross violation of party discipline.

Source: *Delo naroda*, No. 191, 28 October 1917
Published in N D Erofeev, compiler, *Partiya sotsialistov-revolyutsionerov. Dokumenty i materialy. t. 3, ch. 2. Oktyabr' 1917 g. - 1925. g*, ROSSPEN, Moscow, 2003, p. 38.

However much the SR leadership might deplore the "Bolshevik adventure", they very quickly had to face some uncomfortable facts: The Provisional Government had ceased to exist. Almost nobody had rallied to its defence. Much of Russia had no government at all, and there was no chance of constructing one without Bolshevik involvement. The only remotely feasible alternative to Lenin's People's Commissars was the homogenous socialist government advocated by the left wing they had just expelled. In late October and early November 1917, the railway workers' union hosted intensive discussions between different socialist parties on forming a socialist coalition. The People's Socialists, on the far right of narodism, were uncompromisingly hostile.

Document 36. The People's Socialists' CC on agreements with the Bolsheviks

1 November 1917

In its session of 1 November, the CC of the Working People's Socialist Party considered the question of the possibility of constructing a new government based on an agreement between all the socialist parties, including the Bolsheviks. The discussion revealed complete unanimity within the committee. One after another the committee members condemned the Bolsheviks' criminal adventure and predicted its impending bankruptcy. A resolution was passed, with one vote against and two abstentions, which stated that a new government can only be created as a direct successor to the Provisional Government, and that therefore the party categorically rejects any agreements with the Bolsheviks.

Source: *Narodnyy sotsialist* No. 12, 7 November 1917.
Published in A V Sypchenko, K N Morozov (compilers), *Trudovaya Narodno-Sotsialisticheskaya Partiya: dokumenty i materialy*, ROSSPEN, Moscow, 2003, p. 374.

However, the People's Socialists counted for little in Russian politics by this time, and continuity with the Provisional Government would scarcely have been an asset to any administration. Although the railway workers' union negotiations broke down without agreement in early November, the SRs, like the Mensheviks, were prepared to explore all options. As these minutes from the SR CC in November 1917 show, the options considered could be as diverse as coalition with the Bolsheviks on the one hand, and armed resistance on the other.

Document 37. From the minutes of the SR Party CC

14 November 1917

Present: D F Rakov, A Yu Feyt, M Ya Gendel'man, V G Arkhangel'sky, L Ya Gershteyn, M A Vedenyapin, M P Zatonsky, I A Prilezhaev, E S Berg, N I Rakitnikov, V M Zenzinov, V Ya Gurevich

Item: On the organisation of government.
Resolved: That it is essential to form immediately a homogeneous socialist government from representatives of all the socialist parties that accept the following programme:

1. The government is to be organised for the period up to the convocation of the Constituent Assembly, to which all power is to be transferred the moment it opens.

2. The government should be answerable to a National Council, which would be composed of: a) the Central Executive Committee of the Soviet of Workers' and Soldiers' Deputies, supplemented by representatives of those factions which left the All-Russia Congress; b) the same number from the Soviet of Peasants' Deputies, elected at its All-Russia Congress; c) two representatives each from all the socialist parties; d) representatives from the local authorities of the capitals, and e) representatives from the Railway Workers' Union executive and the Postal and Telegraph Union.

3. The dissolution of all military-revolutionary committees, and the restoration of civil liberties.

4. A democratic peace as speedily as possible

5. The democratisation of the army.

6. The abolition of the death penalty

7. The transfer of the land to the land committees.

Item: On sending a delegate to Mogilev.
Resolved: To send a delegation to Mogilev for a meeting of all democratic organisations with a view, should it prove feasible, to organising a new government. The delegation is to consist of L Ya Gersteyn and V G Arkhangel'sky.

17 November 1917

Present: D F Rakov, M A Vedenyapin, V M Zenzinov, A R Gots, M P Zatonsky, E S Berg, I I Teterkin, V Ya Gurevich, A Yu Feyt, M Ya Gendel'man

Item: On the most recent events.
Resolved: Considering that the course of events means that a new civil war is inevitable, and that this war will flare up around the issue of the Constituent Assembly, it is essential to organise all the living forces of the country, armed and unarmed, around the slogans "All Power to the Constituent Assembly" and

"Defence of the Constituent Assembly by all ways and means". A Yu Feyt is to be sent to the front once the attitude of the all-army union has been ascertained. The *stavka* [GHQ] must not fall into the hands of the Bolsheviks, although we cannot ourselves take on the technical aspects of this defence....

Published on http://www.lib.ru/HISTORY/FELSHTINSKY/protokoly_sr.txt

The SRs could do nothing about the *stavka*. On 20 November, General Nikolay Dukhonin was sacked as Commander-in-Chief for refusing to start peace negotiations until there was a functioning central government in Petrograd. What remained of the central command at Mogilev was now headed by the Bolshevik ensign Nikolay Krylenko. The disintegration of the Russian army accelerated. Piece by piece, the state machine that the Constituent Assembly was supposed to inherit was crumbling away.

At the tenth Petrograd conference of SRs in mid-November 1917, Chernov reviewed the illusions and errors of the preceding nine months. Although his criticisms were mainly directed against the right wing of the SR party, they could have been directed with equal justice against Chernov himself – after March he had "adopted the right's position", albeit half-heartedly, and had marked time in an ineffectual coalition government.

Document 38. V M Chernov: The Reasons for the Overturn - from a speech at the 10th Petrograd PSR conference.

15 November 1917

The anarchy which currently reigns in our country is not the fault of the Bolsheviks alone. We have to ask ourselves where the Bolsheviks got the strength not only to embark upon their adventure, but to carry it off successfully. And in listing the reasons, we should not ignore the mistakes of the other side, who were clinging doggedly to ideas which had lost their previous rationale.

When we decided, after the first crisis of the revolutionary government [in April 1917], that it would be possible and useful to join a coalition government, we were guided in particular by two considerations:

1) Before the revolution we had been concerned solely with destroying and overthrowing. We needed to try our hands at positive, constructive work, and

2) We needed to show to the broad masses of the people that we were capable of such work.

Our work in the Provisional Government was supposed to provide the people with an object lesson, to show that it was the representatives of people's Russia, not those of propertied Russia, who deserved all its sympathies.

Then, as our strength and organisation in the country grew, we would be able to increase the extent of our participation and sphere of influence within the government, thereby gradually moving to a homogeneous democratic government. Unfortunately, things turned out differently, and we were not able to realise this programme. Instead of moving forward consistently, at a certain stage we came under the influence of our party's right wing and other elements in the party who had adopted the right's position. We started just marking time. The coalition had already served all its useful purpose, but we kept on reconstructing it, in ever worse and more insipid forms. The supporters of coalition at any price did not want to understand this. Having served its purpose, the coalition form of government became a historical dead weight, and finally an obstacle on the path of historical development.

The last coalition government, as I said when it was formed, was stillborn. It is not surprising that it made mistake after mistake, nor that it was such easy prey for the Bolsheviks. Indeed, for the purposes of their conspiracy, "if such a government had not existed, it would have been necessary to invent it". Nor is it surprising that once it was overthrown, for all its appeals, barely a finger was raised in its defence...

Source: *Delo naroda*, No. 212, 17 November 1917
Published in N D Erofeev, compiler, *Partiya sotsialistov-revolyutsionerov. Dokumenty i materialy. t. 3, ch. 2. Oktyabr' 1917 g. - 1925. g*, ROSSPEN, Moscow, 2003, pp. 50 - 51.

Mikhail Yakovlevich Gendel'man

XII. The Party Splits

Although the SR left and the rest of the party had been at loggerheads for months if not years, neither side had wanted to push the matter as far as a formal split. But the two sides' diametrically opposed reactions to the proclamation of "Soviet power", and the leadership's expulsion of those leftists who had remained at the 2nd Soviet Congress, made further cohabitation all but impossible. The break, however, was not clean. The left SRs called a congress for 17 November (it opened on the 19th) , but still aimed to play a part in the SR party's 4th congress, scheduled to open on 26 November.

Document 39. Radiotelegram of the Left Socialist-Revolutionaries

6 November 1917

To all... to all... to all...

The Central Committee of the Socialist-Revolutionary Party has expelled 176 left Socialist-Revolutionaries from the party for not leaving the 2nd All-Russia Congress of Soviets, to which they had been delegated by local soviets.

The left Socialist-Revolutionaries did not consider it possible to leave the congress, because they recognised it as the authoritative organ of the revolutionary workers, peasants and soldiers. The Petrograd conference and Petrograd organisation of the party protested against these unlawful actions on the part of the Central Committee. In response the Central Committee declared the Petrograd organisation disbanded.

Thus a party split on the eve of the party congress has become a fact. For the time being, until the party congress where this matter will be resolved, all left Socialist-Revolutionaries and their organisations should organise around the left Socialist-Revolutionary fraction of the All-Russia Central Executive Committee of Soviets and around the Petrograd Committee of the Socialist-Revolutionary Party.

The address for contacts and links with the left centre is: Smol'ny Institute, left Socialist-Revolutionary fraction.

The Petrograd committee of left Socialist-Revolutionaries invites comrades to organise, make contact and send people to the all-Russia congress of left Socialist-Revolutionaries called for 17 November. It would be desirable if these delegates were also delegates to the all-party congress.

The platform of the left Socialist-Revolutionaries: the organisation of a government from all socialist parties, a ceasefire on all fronts, negotiations on a democratic peace, the transfer of all land to the land committees pending the Constituent Assembly, the convocation of the Constituent Assembly within the designated time, workers' control of production, the obligation to work etc.

The left Socialist-Revolutionary fraction of the All-Russia Congress
The Petrograd Committee of the Socialist-Revolutionary Party
The All-Russia Military Organisation of Left Socialist-Revolutionaries.

Published in *Znamya truda* No. 64, 6 November 1917
Source: Ya V Leont'ev, compiler, *Partiya levykh sotsialistov-revolyutsionerov, dokumenty i materialy*, Vol. 1, ROSSPEN, Moscow, 2000, p. 62

The parting of the ways was a traumatic experience for many who had devoted their entire lives to the SR party and its cause. Mariya Spiridonova, one of the leaders of the Left SRs, expressed this pain very eloquently. In 1906, at the age of 21, she had assassinated G N Luzhenovsky, a brutal Tsarist official who had been in charge of suppressing peasant unrest in Tambov. She spent the next eleven years in prison and exile, and was only amnestied after the fall of the Tsar. At the first congress of the Left SRs in November 1917, Mariya Spiridonova expressed her bitter disillusionment in the SR leadership since March. Although she did not mention Chernov by name, there is little doubt that he was the main object of her disenchantment, owing to his record of compromise with the right since his return to Russia in April.

Document 40. From Mariya Spiridonova's speech at the 1st congress of the Party of Left Socialist Revolutionaries (Internationalists)

21 November 1917

...The Party of Socialist-Revolutionaries should be working not only for political emancipation, not only for economic emancipation, but also for moral emancipation. Otherwise we become a mere political party, not a party of socialist revolution. This is what has happened in our Central Committee, this narrowing of all our aims into purely political confines. Having become a political party, our party soon became a government party, and having become a government party, it began to justify all the measures of the Provisional Government. Each of us has had the tragic experience of disillusionment in our comrades on the right, whose names for many of us had an aura of sanctity.

I was still just a girl when I first came across our party. And since then I have lived only by those feelings and thoughts which our teachers inculcated in me. On many occasions, in moments of loneliness and despair in distant Siberia, in exile, I drew comfort from remembering that I was not alone, that we still had our fighters out there. On my return from exile, I was full of trepidation at the prospect of meeting our CC. Their names inspired such reverence and delight within me. But, after I had arrived, I gradually came to realise how cruelly mistaken I had been. It is hard for me to convey, comrades, the depths of that disillusionment. Finally I understood that it was all over, there was no possibility of agreement and we had to part....

...We have seen clearly that the past is over and we must separate. Comrades, this has happened because our party had become a party of state and government. We should be especially wary of that – it carries great dangers. We must be first and foremost a socialist party, and only then, if necessary, a political party. Never, at no stage in our struggle, should we enter into agreements with the bourgeoisie.

We should not fear popular movements, uprisings, spontaneous actions, we just need to give them organisation and direction. We are on the threshold of a massive social movement. We will have to travel through many uncharted waters. This means that we have to go along with the Bolsheviks. Although their crude measures are alien to us, we keep close contact with them because the masses have awakened from their torpor and are following them. Maybe the bourgeoisie will smother the class struggle for a while, but that will only be for a while. The struggle will break out again with even greater force, because our economic life has been shaken so much, to its very foundations. The social revolution is maturing, and it will soon break out. We do not just sense this, we can see the signs, we can show it scientifically. Our right-wing comrades do not dispute it. Capitalism has been dealt a heavy blow in our country, the way has been cleared for bringing about socialism. In Western Europe all the material conditions are present, but they lack the ideology to inspire them. We have a lot of that ideology. Victory must come to the working masses – indeed never before in history have such broad masses of workers been brought into struggle. But victory will be assured if it goes under the banner of the International. But some other words must also be inscribed on the International's banners: "fraternity, love and trust". If we rally under that banner, we shall be invincible, comrades!

Source: *Protokoly pervogo s"ezda Partii levykh sotsialistov-revolyutsionerov (internatsionalistov)*, Revolyutsionnyy sotsializm, Moscow, 1918.
Published in Ya V Leont'ev, compiler, *Partiya levykh sotsialistov-revolyutsionerov, dokumenty i materialy*, Vol. 1, ROSSPEN, Moscow, 2000, pp. 96 – 97.

For his part, Chernov almost certainly had Spiridonova, among others, in mind when a few days later, at the 4th congress of the main SR party, he spoke of a "Golgothist" current of heroic but futile self-sacrifice among the Left SRs.

Document 41. From V M Chernov's speech to the 4th congress of the SR party

26 November 1917

...A certain group of people who still consider themselves to be socialist-revolutionaries have been adopting the Bolsheviks' positions. In fact they have simply become maximalists, but they were able to leave us and go over to the Bolsheviks, to an alliance with the Bolsheviks. ... But I should note an exception. Besides maximalism in an SR sauce, there is another ideological current. I spent a long time trying to find an exact description of it, an exact name for it, but then I found one in various articles in *Znamya truda*. To use their term for it, this current can be called "Golgothism", from the word Golgotha. These people exist, and some of them continue to call themselves socialist-revolutionaries. They say, quite definitely and honestly, that Russia is, of course, not ready for reconstructing on socialist lines. Any attempt to force a socialist reconstruction, a maximalist revolution, is doomed to failure, to perish. But what else can one do, when the countries that are more ready for socialism are living under the nightmare of war and cannot cast off their chains, while the most backward country has found itself in the vanguard of the revolution? And so, although disaster is inevitable, they must climb the Golgotha of history, they must strain every nerve in heroic efforts to make a maximalist social revolution. So what if it all ends in disaster here, in Russia, if the revolution is drowned, if it is overrun by civil war? If it can "hang on" for long enough, and its example can shake the social consciousness of the proletarian masses in the West and bring about revolutions over there, then the job is done. The Russian revolution will fall, but it will be the sacrifice which will redeem Europe and the whole world! The revolution will be crucified, the Russian people will bear the cross, and though they may themselves perish, they will give eternal life to others.

This is the romantic fairy-tale they offer instead of a theory, in which the main lever of historical progress is the example – a hopeless example, which just has to "hang on" for a certain time to have its effect. It is assumed in all this that the better-prepared countries will not appreciate that this revolution is hopeless, that it is doomed.

This is the pseudotheory that drives this maximalism in SR sauce. It may contain a lot of poetry, and a lot of the Christian spirit of martyrdom, but it lacks any analysis of the historical situation, and as political thought it lacks even the most elementary clarity and common sense.

Source: *Kratkiy otchet o rabotakh chetvertogo s"ezda partii s.-r.*, Petrograd, 1918
Published in N D Erofeev, compiler, *Partiya sotsialistov-revolyutsionerov. Dokumenty i materialy. t. 3, ch. 2. Oktyabr' 1917 g. - 1925. g*, ROSSPEN, Moscow, 2003, pp. 72 – 73.

XIII. The All-Russia Constituent Assembly

The final split in the SR party occurred just after the long-postponed elections to the Constituent Assembly, which were held over most of the country on 12 November 1917. The electoral lists, which had been drawn up by the party leaderships in the different electoral districts, had been finalised some time before the polls. In the case of the SRs, in most places there was just one SR list, drawn up before the split, on which leftists were in a minority. Conversely, in those areas where the SR organisation had been dominated by the left before the split, the party list was mainly leftist. As for the outcome of the elections, of the 707 deputies identified, 370 were SRs, including 80 or so Ukrainian SRs, 40 were Left SRs, 175 were Bolsheviks. The Mensheviks, who had largely determined the politics of the SR-Menshevik bloc in the Soviets, were all but wiped out – they got just 16 seats, mainly from Georgia. The People's Socialists managed only two seats.

It is impossible to tell how far the results would have differed had there been separate SR and Left SR lists across Russia, and their largely peasant electorate had been given the choice between them. But their poor showing made the Left SRs more inclined to the Bolshevik view that the only useful purpose the Constituent Assembly could serve would be to grant its seal of approval to Soviet power. At the Left SR founding congress in November, the lawyer Aleksandr Shreyder made a legal case for disregarding the assembly if the need arose.

Document 42. 1st Congress of Left SRs: Report of comrade A A Shreyder on "The Constituent Assembly"

28 November 1917

When I hear the call "All Power to the Constituent Assembly", which is now so fashionable, I realise that people are not taking stock of what it is they are demanding.

Can unconditional, unlimited power really, in actual fact, belong to the Constituent Assembly? Are its rights and areas of competence not limited by certain norms which it cannot exceed? Or does Russia lie before it as some kind of *tabula rasa*, on which the Constituent Assembly can sketch out the most intricate designs?

I shall try to answer these questions from a social and legal point of view.

The revolutionary drama always consists of three acts. The first is the most active, the most difficult – the plot, the seizure of power, the uprising. In the second, the action reaches its culmination. It is in essence the centrepiece and sense of the entire drama, in which the whole people recognises the new power. Finally, in the third act, there is the development of the revolutionary drama, the transformation of temporary authorities into permanent ones, operating in accordance with certain, "constitutional" legal norms.

The Russian revolution has passed through the first two acts and now stands on the threshold of the third.

The second period could have ended naturally and painlessly with the Constituent Assembly. It should have happened in June or July [1917]. Then the revolutionary cycle would have been completed and peaceful constructive work could have begun.

But things turned out differently. The second period was full of the most unexpected disturbances. Again we came to the conclusion – a new rising which marks a new phase in the development of the revolution.

The Constituent Assembly – this Constituent Assembly – has come too late. It cannot have its original all-embracing significance. It is constrained by the real gains of the revolution.

So what does "All Power to the Constituent Assembly" mean now? Or, to put it in more concrete terms, let us ask: how far should the legal enactments of the revolutionary period be obligatory for the Constituent Assembly? To what extent are the laws and decrees of the revolutionary government effective?

If the Constituent Assembly is to exist, it will, of course, be able to publish new laws and, consequently, repeal old ones. But that is not the question. It is much deeper.

Can the Constituent Assembly, by annulling a law, thereby annul the consequences of its operation by those with an interest in it? Can the Constituent Assembly rule that all actions based on the laws and decrees of the revolutionary government are null and void, that they did not take place? Only if we answer that question in the affirmative can we say "All Power to the Constituent Assembly"....

Let us imagine that the law on the socialisation of land is repealed by a new law from the Constituent Assembly. There is no way that the land that has legally passed into common use could be returned. The peasants, having socialised a piece of land, were acting according to the specific instructions of a law which may be repealed, but may certainly not be regarded as null and void.

If this is the case – and in any other case a structured social existence would be impossible – then what sense is there in the loud calls for "All Power to the Constituent Assembly"? Is it not just empty noise?

The Constituent Assembly's power is entirely constrained on all sides by the real concrete gains of the revolution. Governmental changes and fluctuations are possible only within the confines of those gains.

This juridical analysis confirms the attitude we have always taken to the expression of the people's will, whatever form it takes. Following the precepts of narodism, we have always put the interests of the people first, not the opinions of the people. Of course, as democrats, we base ourselves on the people's will, but it is not our foundation stone. My class ego, my subjective ego may act as its guardian, its executor, and its censor. Under what circumstances does my ego have the right and duty to pronounce its categorical subjective "no"? Where is the criterion which sets the boundaries of the power of the "will of the people"?

... For us, socialist-revolutionaries, this criterion is the well-being of real people and the interests of international labour solidarity.

The Constituent Assembly can and should get our support only insofar as it defends these social values.

In contrast, Perets Shifer from Odessa saw no good reason to abandon the hallowed SR position on the Constituent Assembly.

Document 43. 1st Congress of Left SRs: Contribution of P Shifer on "The Constituent Assembly"

28 November 1917

Ever since the proclamation of the dictatorship of the Soviets, the transfer of all power to the Soviets, we have started to reject the Constituent Assembly. At first we were against transferring power to the Soviets, both at the III party congress, and at the Democratic Conference. Immediately after the October overturn we were calling for a homogeneous socialist government. But now we have abandoned our positions to proclaim, along with the Bolsheviks, "All Power to the Soviets".

But did we have grounds for changing our position? What has changed? Nothing. If the dictatorship of the Soviets really were possible, we would not have all this anarchy and sabotage. Essentially, we have no government at all now. What is Soviet power, and who recognises it, apart from those who regard it as the socialist revolution? Only comrade Ustinov and 2 or 3 others are convinced that the socialist revolution has arrived. So long as we are not advocating the immediate introduction of socialism, we have nothing to fear from the Constituent Assembly. It will be socialist and will implement our minimum programme. And if this is the case, then, comrades, you should say "All Power to the Constituent Assembly". There is now a different danger – the danger that the assembly could be wrecked. This is already a real threat. And we now face the prospect of civil war. At this point we, socialist revolutionaries, should stand firmly on our own feet and not be dragged along on the tails of the Bolsheviks.

An altogether harder line was put by Prosh Prosh'yan, who had been expelled from the SR party in July 1917 for his support for the "July days" demonstrations.

Document 44. 1st Congress of Left SRs: Contribution of P P Prosh'yan on "The Constituent Assembly"

28 November 1917

If we see and believe that the social revolution has begun, then power belongs to the Soviets of Workers', Soldiers' and Peasants' Deputies. If not, then power belongs to the Constituent Assembly. At present real power is in the hands of the workers' democracy, and that power was won after massive struggles with the bourgeoisie. Of course, we cannot and must not surrender it to the Constituent Assembly and lay down our arms. Therefore, if the Constituent Assembly tries to organise a government as its first act, then conflict with the Soviets is inevitable. If it wants to take power into its own hands, we will not give up that power.

Sources for documents 42-44: *Protokoly pervogo s''ezda Partii levykh sotsialistov-revolyutsionerov (internatsionalistov)*, Revolyutsionnyy sotsializm, Moscow, 1918.
Published in Ya V Leont'ev (compiler), *Partiya levykh sotsialistov-revolyutsionerov: dokumenty i materialy*, Vol. 1. ROSSPEN, Moscow, 2000, pp. 164, 167, 168.

For the main SR party, the Constituent Assembly was their last hope. The Soviet government had held the elections on the appointed date, 12 November. However, since supporters of Soviet power turned out to be in a minority among the deputies, Lenin's government did not allow the assembly to open on the scheduled date of 28 November. Over six weeks it used various delaying tactics, including setting quorums of delegates, introducing Soviet-type rules permitting re-election of assembly deputies, and arresting those deputies who tried to convene the assembly on the scheduled date. The SR CC was reduced to a state of impotent fury.

Document 45. From the Central Committee of the PSR to the whole working people of Russia

Petrograd, December 1917

Comrade workers, peasants and soldiers!

Two months have passed since the Bolshevik party seized power in this country.

Making use of the mistakes of the last government, having lured the people with enticing promises, the Bolsheviks seized power by armed force, on which they continue to rely.

The time has now come to take stock of what they have given us in their two months in charge of the country, and whether they have fulfilled their promises to the people.

They promised us bread, but we are now on the verge of a complete famine.

They promised to reduce food prices, but prices are rising and pillaging has reached unprecedented levels.

They promised to give land, but instead they just issued a decree repeating a resolution of the peasants' deputies drafted by the Socialist-Revolutionaries. In the countryside land is just being seized, and the wealth which should belong to the whole working people is being grabbed by whoever is the strongest.

They promised the workers order in the factories and the development of industry through workers' control, but plants and factories are closing down everywhere and the army of unemployed is growing.

They promised an immediate general, people's, just peace, but they are concluding it with hostile states, conducting negotiations with them in secret and separately from the Allies, and now they themselves have recognised that the peace the enemy has offered them is unacceptable.

The army, hungry and cold, is deserting the front, and the Germans, for all their fine words about peace, know that Russia is in their hands and they can do whatever they want with her.

They are concluding peace with the enemy whilst starting wars within Russia, against the Don, the Urals, and the fraternal Ukrainian people, infringing their freedom and independence.

They promised freedom and order, but they are silencing everyone, banning meetings, closing papers, and introducing controls over the press just like under the Tsar.

They do not trust the people, they consider the people to be unenlightened. They are spending the nation's money on distributing only their own papers, while destroying the others. They want the whole people to see things through their eyes.

They abolish the death penalty at the front, but introduce it in the rear. They have destroyed the courts, but have brought in kangaroo courts.

Never before, especially in the towns, has life been as terrifying as it is now that power and order are in the hands of the Bolsheviks, with its flagrant robberies, incessant shooting, and drunken riots.

They are arresting socialists and revolutionaries, filling the prisons with them, while freeing the Dubrovins, Beletskies, Kurlovs and other Black Hundreds.

The call themselves a workers' and peasants' government, but take no account of the soviets of workers' and peasants' deputies. They do not answer to them, but instead just cause splits and discord. At the centre of power they have put persons who are mostly unknown to the people, incompetent, plain rogues and swindlers, who should themselves be removed and arrested for bribery and corruption before a few weeks has passed.

The state is disintegrating, the country is dying, and the supporters of the old order are stirring again. They see the destruction and internecine strife as the guarantee of their impending victory, and are already thinking of restoring the power of the Tsars.

But the Bolsheviks, regarding themselves as the sole defenders of the people, slander the other socialist parties, fling dirt at them, spread lies about them, whilst strengthening the people's enemies by their actions.

Imagining that they can bring about socialism with bayonets and violence, they are destroying everything that the people have achieved so far.

Comrades! You can all see where Bolshevik rule leads. There is but one hope left for the people – the Constituent Assembly. The people have struggled for it for many long years, they have been thinking about it for nine months now, they are waiting for it to resolve all the questions of their working lives.

Before they seized power, the Bolsheviks screamed loudest of all that the capitalists were delaying the convocation of the Constituent Assembly and wanted to wreck it. They promised to convene it immediately. It is already three weeks past the date for convening it, and the "People's Commissars" have not only not opened it, but are not even allowing the deputies to go there. They are arresting the deputies, using force against them, and declaring that they will disperse the Constituent Assembly if it does not defer to the Commissars. They have called the Latvian regiments to Petrograd for the purpose of dispersing the Assembly. They are trying to slander the non-Bolshevik deputies in any way they can, and to deceive the people by saying that the Constituent Assembly is full of enemies of the people who have got in there under false pretences. As everyone now knows, capitalists will comprise no more than one twentieth of the Constituent Assembly, and power will be in safe hands. But the Bolsheviks want to foist their will upon everyone by force. Ensign Krylenko in his orders to the army has called directly for an armed assault on the Constituent Assembly. "Do not let your arms waver", he says, "if you have to raise them against the deputies."

Comrades! You can see how the Bolsheviks are carrying out their promises. Look at our life today and judge honestly – has it got better, or are we heading for ruin? Our only salvation lies in transferring all power to the Constituent Assembly, which will rule the country with the consent and support of the whole revolutionary people. It will restore order, conclude peace, issue a proper law on transferring the land to the people, and put and end to the industrial chaos.

Only the Constituent Assembly can give the country peace, because only it can represent all of Russia, as it was elected by the whole people using the fairest electoral law.

Only the Constituent Assembly can be the uncontested legal authority, whose right to speak in the name of Russia is recognised equally within Russia and without, both by our enemies and our allies. All the Bolsheviks can offer is either an obscene peace or a hopeless prolongation of the war.

Only the Constituent Assembly, by properly formulated legislation, can give the land to the working people without compensation, on an equal basis for those who work it. In the chaos and anarchy created by the Bolsheviks, those who want to get rich are grabbing the land.

Only the Constituent Assembly can put a stop to the chaos in industry and on the railways and end hunger.

Only the Constituent Assembly can stop the internecine civil war criminally instigated by the Bolsheviks to the delight of the Germans and the Black Hundreds.

Meet in your factories, your village assemblies, your barracks, consider the situation, draft your resolutions and verdicts, and demand the immediate convocation of the Constituent Assembly and that all power be given to it. Prepare right away to defend it from the Bolsheviks, do not let them use violence against the people's elected representatives – otherwise the country will perish, along with all your hopes and aspirations.

Source: Marc Jansen, ed., *The Socialist-Revolutionary Party after October 1917. Documents from the P.S.-R. Archives*, Stichting Beheer IISG, Amsterdam, 1989, pp. 27 - 30.

Eventually, the Soviet government fixed a date for the Constituent Assembly to open – 5 January 1918. Two days beforehand, on 3 January, the Soviet Central Executive Committee adopted a "Declaration of Rights of the Working and Exploited People", which declared as its first point: "Russia is hereby proclaimed a Republic of Soviets of Workers' Soldiers' and Peasants' Deputies. All power, centrally and locally, is vested in these Soviets".* The Assembly was to be invited to endorse this declaration. If it did so, it rendered itself redundant. If it did not, then the real balance of forces within Russia would be tested.

And so, the long-awaited Constituent Assembly opened at 4.00 p.m. on 5 January, in the Tauride Palace in Petrograd. Almost immediately, the Bolshevik Yakov Sverdlov from the Soviet CEC read out the Soviet declaration and recommended it to the Assembly. The first trial of strength concerned the election of a chairperson. The Bolsheviks and Left SRs proposed Mariya Spiridonova, the mainstream SRs proposed Viktor Chernov. Chernov was elected by 244 votes to 153. In a chaotic session, interrupted by insults traded between deputies and catcalls from the public galleries, the majority resolved not to debate the Soviet declaration. F F Raskol'nikov, for the Bolsheviks, denounced the majority as "enemies of the people" and led his faction out of the chamber.**

The Left SRs did not follow suit immediately. Isaak Shteynberg, at that time the Left SR Commissar of Justice in Lenin's government, goaded his former party comrades, daring them to come out openly against Soviet policies.

Document 46. From I Z Shteynberg's speech at the Constituent Assembly

6 January 1918

"...We expected that the Constituent Assembly would have to reveal its socio-political face to the country. But this Constituent Assembly, in the shape of its right-wing majority, has shied away from that task today. It has not dared to rise up against Soviet power immediately. The right majority of our present Constituent Assembly has not dared to rise up against the existing Soviet government. It has shrunk away from stating definitely where it stands on the programme that Soviet power has worked out and is carrying out. It did not dare reject the CEC programme, but it managed to shy away from putting a discussion

---

* See Yuri Akhapkin, compiler, *First Decrees of Soviet Power*, Lawrence & Wishart, London, 1970, p. 76.
** See T E Novitskaya, compiler, *Uchreditel'noe sobranie. Rossiya. 1918 g.*, Nedra, Moscow, 1991, p. 141.

of that programme onto the agenda. The Bolshevik Party and the party of their closest comrades and friends consider that enough to show the people the truth about this matter. In our view, this refusal to put the question for discussion means that the right majority in the Constituent Assembly has told the country clearly and unambiguously: "We are not with the Soviets, we are against the Soviets, we want to construct some kind of state machine of our own to deal a death blow against the gains of the people's revolution." But although we are in complete agreement with our comrades, the Bolshevik Assembly deputies, on this basic political question, we are going to take one last step ... we are going to say: "You have avoided stating your position on the whole programme, so please be so good as to state today, in this hall, before we break up, your attitude to the foreign policy, the policy on war and peace pursued by the Soviet government." We are presenting this part of the CEC resolution, dealing with the peace policy of the present Soviet government, as an ultimatum to you. We are saying openly – if you stand for Soviet power, if you recognise the workers' gains of the October revolution, then you will not dare to go against this point, which I shall now read out to you.... "Expressing firm determination to wrest mankind from the clutches of finance capital and imperialism, which have in this most criminal of wars drenched the world in blood, the Constituent Assembly unreservedly endorses the Soviet policy of denouncing the secret treaties, organising most extensive fraternisation with the workers and peasants of the combatant armies and achieving at all costs by revolutionary means a democratic peace for the working people, without annexations or reparations, on the basis of the free self-determination of nations." We propose that this motion put by the Left SRs be adopted today, before we leave this hall. If this motion is rejected, then the current make-up of the Constituent Assembly, and the need to break with that assembly, will become clear not only to the Left SR faction, but to the whole mass of the people of the Russian republic.

Source: T E Novitskaya, compiler, *Uchreditel'noe sobranie. Rossiya. 1918 g.*, Nedra, Moscow, 1991, pp. 143 – 144.

When the assembly refused to rise to that bait, Vladimir Karelin led the Left SR faction out of the hall. At last, all the procedural wrangling was over, and, in the early hours of 6 January, Viktor Chernov was able to propose the SRs' own land law for the Russian republic. He had been waiting for this moment for his whole political life. But he surely cannot have imagined that it would turn out like this.

Document 47. V M Chernov's draft land law, presented at the Constituent Assembly.

6 January 1918

Chairman [V M Chernov]: Permit me to read out the "Draft basic law on land", put forward by the SR fraction.

1. Property rights in land within the Russian Republic are henceforth abolished forever.

2. All land located within the Russian Republic, with all its mineral wealth, forests and waters are national property.

3. The right of disposal of all land with its minerals, forests and waters belongs to the republic in the person of its central and local government organs on the basis laid down by this law.

4. Regions of the Russian Republic which are juridically self-governing will exercise their rights over the land on the basis of this law and in accordance with the federal constitution.

5. The aims of the state authorities in distributing the land, mineral wealth, forests and waters are: a) the creation of conditions which favour the best use of the country's natural resources and the highest development of productive forces and b) a just distribution of all natural wealth amongst the population.

6. Individuals and institutions may only exercise usufructory rights over land, mineral resources, forests and waters.

7. Any citizen of the Russian Republic, regardless of nationality or belief, groups of citizens, as well as state and social institutions, may use land, mineral resources, forests and waters.

8. Usufructory land rights are acquired, exercised and terminated in accordance with the principles laid down in this basic law.

9. Land rights currently belonging to individuals, groups and institutions, insofar as they contradict this law, are revoked.

10. The transfer to public property of land, mineral wealth, forests and waters currently held by individuals, groups or institutions as property or under another law of estate, will take place without compensation.

Citizen sailor [A G Zheleznyakov]: I have been instructed to inform you that everyone present should vacate the hall, because the guard is tired. (Voices: "We don't need any guard!")

Chairman: What instruction? From whom?

Citizen sailor: I am the head of the Tauride Palace guard, and have instructions from Commissar Dybenko.

Chairman: All members of the Constituent Assembly are also very tired, but tiredness must not interrupt the proclamation of the land law for which all Russia has been waiting. (Dreadful noise. Shouts of "Enough! enough!") The Constituent Assembly can only be dispersed if force is used. (Noise. Voices: "Down with Chernov!")

Citizen sailor: [inaudible] ...I request that you vacate the hall immediately.

Source: T E Novitskaya, compiler, *Uchreditel'noe sobranie. Rossiya. 1918 g.*, Nedra, Moscow, 1991, pp. 158 – 159.

Viktor Mikhaylovich Chernov

XIV. Epilogue

At 4.40 a.m. on 6 January 1918, Chernov declared the session closed, to be resumed at 5.00 p.m. later that day. When the deputies returned to continue their deliberations, the Tauride Palace was locked.

The Socialist-Revolutionaries never recovered from the dispersal of the Constituent Assembly. They had won an election only to find they had lost a state. Their responses to this new and unfamiliar situation were varied. "Soviet power" was not established throughout Russia for several months after the overturn in Petrograd, and in many places SRs remained in control of local administrations. In the areas under Bolshevik control the main SR party tried to maintain its legal existence.

A few members and associates of the party attempted to revive the old tactic of assassination: on 20 June 1918 the Bolshevik press commissar Volodarsky was shot by a Petersburg worker, the SR Sergeev, although this act was disavowed by the SR CC. On 30 August 1918 the poet Leonid Kanegisser, a People's Socialist, assassinated the Petrograd Cheka head Moysey Uritsky, while Fania Kaplan, an anarchist-communist in league with various SR elements, shot and wounded Lenin in Moscow. The Bolsheviks' response to this – a furious Red Terror – demonstrated how counterproductive such tactics were.

When the British intervened in the North of Russia, some SRs played a role in the local "white" administration there. Some still clung to the hope that the Constituent Assembly – *their* Constituent Assembly – could be revived. In June 1918 a "Committee of Members of the Constituent Assembly" (*Komuch*) was formed in Samara, following the overthrow of the Bolshevik administration there by Czechoslovak troops. Headed by the SR V K Vol'sky, it took power locally. By early autumn it had gathered almost 100 Assembly delegates from across Russia, declared itself to be the legitimate government of the whole country and tried to extend its influence to all parts of Russia not controlled by the Bolsheviks. In September it took part in a conference in Ufa which created a "Provisional All-Russian Government", and a Directory of five, three of whom were SRs or SR supporters. This arrangement lasted just six weeks. In November 1918 Admiral Kolchak, who had no love for socialists of any stripe, arrested the SR members and established his own dictatorship, of a more pronounced right-wing authoritarian character. In the political polarisation of the Russian civil war, there was little space for moderate "democratic" socialists on either side of the front lines. Under such circumstances, the overwhelming majority of SRs simply abandoned political activity altogether.

The Left SRs on the other hand, flourished for a brief period. They predominated at the Extraordinary All-Russia Congress of Soviets of Peasant Deputies in November 1917. Although they could not use this as a lever to take power, they were represented in the Council of People's Commissars from December 1917 until March 1918. Left SR support played an important role in securing peasant acceptance of Soviet government in the early period – there were very few Bolsheviks in rural areas, and so for the first few months "Soviet power" in the villages meant

"Left SR power". The Left SRs withdrew from the central Soviet government in protest against the Brest-Litovsk peace treaty with Germany, which involved major territorial and financial concessions to Germany. However, Left SR representatives remained in local Soviet administrations, and in the Cheka, the secret police, until July 1918. On 6 July, V A Aleksandrovich, a Left SR and one of F E Dzerzhinsky's deputies, used his Cheka position to facilitate the assassination of Count Mirbach, the German ambassador. Thereafter the main body of Left SRs was also subject to state persecution, while the more pro-Bolshevik of them formed ever smaller political grouplets, such as Kolegaev and Natanson's short-lived "Party of Revolutionary Communism". Most of these little parties were absorbed into the Bolshevik party between 1918 and 1920.

The main SR party in the Bolshevik-controlled Russian heartland was heavily repressed, although up to 1920 it was occasionally permitted to publish a newspaper or send a token representation to a congress of Soviets. It continued to play a role on the periphery – the "Irkutsk political centre" in Siberia which organised the successful rising against the white Admiral Kolchak in January 1920 was an SR-dominated body. Within three weeks, however, it had surrendered power in that part of Siberia to the Bolsheviks.

SR ideas continued to have influence among the peasantry, and individual current and former party members were involved in several peasant rebellions against the Bolsheviks' food-requisitioning brigades in the closing stages of the civil war. The most important of these rebellions was the Tambov rising of 1920-22, led by a former Left SR, A S Antonov. The rebels' organisation, the "Union of Toiling Peasants", issued leaflets and a programme with a strongly narodnik-socialist flavour. This local civil war was fought with desperate ferocity on both sides, until the rebellion was eventually crushed, with considerable brutality, by Red Army commander M N Tukhachevsky.

The *coup de grâce* to the SR party as an organisation within Soviet Russia was delivered in the form of a show-trial in 1922. The trial was not an unqualified success for the Soviet government. The SR leaders in the dock refused to admit their guilt. They defended themselves and their party with great dignity, and tried as far as they could to turn the proceedings into a trial of their accusers. Internationally, the main outcome of this judicial farce was a further deterioration in Soviet relations with non-communist workers' parties across the globe.

At the same time, thousands of former SRs who had abandoned politics and any kind of opposition activity remained at liberty in the USSR in the 1920s. Many of them even held responsible positions in state, co-operative or agrarian institutions. The most notable example was the brilliant economist Nikolay Kondrat'ev, who headed the Conjuncture Institute, an economic forecasting body, and was prominent in the Commissariat of Agriculture until his arrest in 1930. However, even this limited tolerance did not last long. Later that decade, former members of the SR party, left or right, were very vulnerable to arrest.

As for narodnik socialism as a world view, it was finally killed off in its land of origin by the forcible collectivisation of agriculture after 1929. Stolypin's agrarian reforms before World War 1 had been intended to destroy peasant radicalism by enhancing (some) peasants' individual economic independence. Stalin's agrarian reforms took the opposite approach. They crushed peasant radicalism far more effectively by eliminating the peasants' economic independence entirely.

XV. Biographical index

Aksakov, Konstantin Sergeevich, (1817 – 1860). Journalist, poet, literary critic, historian, leading Slavophile ideologist. **61**

Aleksandrovich Petr, (Dmitrievsky V. A., 1884 – 1918). Worker, internationalist SR during war, one of the Left SR leaders 1917 - 1918. Deputy chairman of All-Russian Cheka 1918, involved in Left SR rising 6.7.1918. Executed without trial 7.7.1918. **98**

Alekseev, Mikhail Vasil'evich, (1857 – 1918). General. Commanded various fronts in WW1, August 1915 appointed Chief of Staff of C-in-C. February 1917 helped persuade Nicholas to abdicate. 11.3.1917 – 22.5.1917 – C-in-C. 1.9.1917 arrested Kornilov although sympathised with him. Formed anti-Red armies straight after October 1917. Died of heart disease. **15**

Alexander II (Romanov, Aleksandr Nikolaevich, 1818 – 1881). Emperor from 1855. Early reign included notable liberal reforms: ended serfdom 1861, introduced limited elected local government 1864 and 1870, reformed legal system 1864, etc., but defended autocracy. Assassinated by *Narodnaya volya.* **8**

Alexander III (Romanov, Aleksandr Aleksandrovich 1845 – 1894). Emperor from 1881. Hostile to father's liberal course, rolled back certain reforms, strengthened autocratic and caste principles in administration. Died of nephritis and excessive drinking. **8**

Antonov, Aleksandr Stepanovich (1889 – 1922). Tambov peasant leader. SR-Maximalist from 1906, in internal exile 1907-17. Headed Kirsanov *uezd* police 1917. Led Tambov peasants' rising against Bolsheviks 1920-20. Shot by GPU. **98**

Arkhangel'sky, Vasiliy Gavrilovich, (1868 – 1948). SR deputy in 2nd State Duma 1907, writer, lecturer, on SR CC 1917. Later in emigration, Prague. **80**

Avksent'ev, Nikolay Dmitrievich (1878 – 1943). SR leader. In Petrograd Soviet 1905, exiled north of Arctic Circle, escaped abroad 1907. Favoured legal party work and abandonment of terrorism. Defencist in war, returned to Russia after February 1917, chaired All-Russia Soviet of Peasant Deputies. July - September 1917 - Minister of Internal Affairs. Member of "Provisional All-Russia Government" in Ufa, 1918. Deposed by Kolchak, emigrated. **11, 28-29, 31**

Azef, Evno Fishelevich, (1869 – 1918). Police agent from 1893, SR from 1899, headed SR Fighting Organisation 1903 – 1908. Organised assassinations of officials. Exposed as police agent 1908, fled abroad. Interned as enemy alien in Germany 1915, died shortly after release. **10-11, 32**

Batrak (Zatonsky, Mikhail Petrovich, 1882 – ?). Worker, SR, on Petersburg Soviet 1905, on SR CC 1917. Arrested 1920. Accused in 1922 SR show trial. Fate unknown. **24, 80**

Beletsky, Stepan Petrovich, (1873 – 1918). Tsarist state functionary and police chief. Head of Police Department 1912-14. Senator from 1914. Arrested March 1917, transferred to Moscow end 1917, shot in Red Terror. **91**

Berg, Efroim Solomonovich, (1875 – 1937). SR, on Petrograd Soviet and Soviet CEC 1917. Arrested several times after 1918. Sentenced to prison after SR show trial

1922. In prison and exile until shot 1937. **80**

Bogrov, Dmitriy Georgievich, (1887 – 1911). Son of Kiev lawyer, revolutionary, police agent. Social-democrat 1905, SR-Maximalist from 1906, anarchist-communist and police informer from 1907. Assassinated P A Stolypin 1911. Tried and hanged. **11**

Bol'shakov. SR, on Petrograd Soviet 1917. **24**

Breshko-Breshkovskaya, Ekaterina Konstantinovna, (1844 – 1934). Narodnik from 1870s, founder member of SR party. Known as "grandmother of the revolution" in 1917. On right of party, unconditional supporter of Kerensky. Emigrated 1919. **11**

Broydo, Mark Isaevich (Mordukh Mendel'evich, 1877 – 1937). Social-democrat from 1900, Menshevik from 1904, defencist in WW1, on Petrograd Soviet EC 1917. Opposed all compromise with Bolsheviks after October 1917. Emigrated 1919. **28**

Brusilov, Aleksey Alekseevich, (1853 – 1926). Professional soldier, General from 1912, commander in WW1, led offensives 1916 and 1917. Hostile to Bolsheviks, but did not join Whites. In Red Army from 1920. **52**

Chaadaev, Petr Yakovlevich, (1794 – 1856). Russian aristocrat, Catholic-influenced philosopher. Joined Decembrist revolutionaries 1821, but abroad at time of rising 1825. Sharply criticised effect of Orthodoxy on Russia in journal *Teleskop*, 1836. Declared insane by government. **62-63**

Chernov, Viktor Mikhaylovich, (1873 – 1952). SR leader and theoretician. In revolutionary peasant-socialist movement from 1890s, one of SR party founders, on CC throughout, wrote SR programme. Internationalist in WW1. Returned from emigration April 1917, agriculture minister in Provisional Government summer 1917. January 1918 elected chairman of Constituent Assembly. Favoured resisting Bolsheviks. Briefly led *Komuch* at Ufa until Kolchak's coup, November 1918. Thereafter favoured peace with Bolsheviks and resistance to Kolchak. Lived underground in Moscow 1919, emigrated to Prague 1920, led SR delegation abroad. Died in USA. **9, 11-12, 27-28, 30-32, 48, 51-54, 65-66, 81-82, 84-86, 93-97**

Chikhachev. Petrograd SR, 1917. **25**

Chkheidze, Nikolay Semenovich, (1864 – 1926). Social-democrat from 1892, in RSDRP from 1898. Led Menshevik group in 3rd and 4th State Dumas. Internationalist in WW1. Chaired Petrograd Soviet March–September 1917, opposed joining Provisional Government May 1917. After October moved to Georgia, chaired Georgian Constituent Assembly, favoured Georgian independence. Emigrated 1921, committed suicide in Paris. **28**

Dostoevsky, Fedor Mikhaylovich, (1821 – 1881). Writer, most famous for *Crime and Punishment*, (1866). First works published 1846, 1849 arrested for involvement in Petrashevtsy socialist circle, imprisoned and exiled to Siberia, later amnestied. Abandoned socialism for monarchism and Orthodoxy, argued Russia's uniqueness. **60, 62**

Dubrovin, Aleksandr Ivanovich, (1855 – 1921?). Extreme reactionary Russian nationalist, anti-Semite, pogromist. Former army doctor. Believed revolutionary movement to be a Jewish conspiracy. Founder of Black Hundred "Union of the Russian People" 1905. Arrested after February 1917, released on health grounds shortly before Bolshevik takeover. Arrested by Cheka 1920, tried and shot. **91**

Dukhonin, Nikolay Nikolaevich, (1876 – 1917). Professional soldier, General in WW1, appointed Chief of Staff September 1917. After flight of Kerensky 26.10.1917, became C-in-C. Refused Bolshevik order to start peace negotiations. Released Kornilov plotters 19.11.1917, replaced by Krylenko 20.11.1917, seized and beaten to death by sailors. **81**

Dybenko, Pavel Efimovich, (1889 – 1938). Bolshevik from 1912, Baltic sailor in WW1, arrested for anti-war activity. In Petrograd MRC October 1917, then in Lenin's government, People's Commissar for Navy 1918. Sacked and expelled from party for losing battle of Narva, 1918, restored 1922. In Red Army organisation and command posts. Arrested and shot 1938. **95**

Dzerzhinsky, Feliks Edmundovich, (1877 – 1926). Social-democrat from 1895, follower of Rosa Luxemburg. Exiled and imprisoned in Russia. Freed 1.3.1917 from Butyrki prison by soldiers. Active in Moscow and Petrograd, involved in Bolshevik seizure of power. From 7.12.1917 head of Cheka, organised Red Terror. Held other party and state posts, from 1924 also head of Supreme Economic Council. **98**

Fedorov, General. Chairman of Military League, 1917. **65**

Feyt, Andrey Yul'evich, (1864 – 1926). Revolutionary from 1882, doctor, founder member of SRs. Arrested several times. On SR CC from 1905. Escaped abroad from internal exile 1907. Volunteer doctor in French army from 1914. After February 1917 on EC of Petrograd Soviet and SR CC. Abandoned politics after 1918. Witness at SR show trial 1922. **80-81**

Filippovsky, Vasiliy Nikolaevich, (1889 – 1940). SR since 1903. Arrested and exiled. In WW1 – Naval Lieutenant. On Petrograd Soviet EC from March 1917 and Soviet CEC from June. Among organisers of Petrograd's defence against Kornilov, August. Constituent Assembly deputy. 1918 worked in metalworkers' union. Joined *Komuch* in Samara, June 1918. Lived underground to 1920. Arrested by Cheka 1921, defence witness in SR trial 1922. Then in prison and exile, died in camps. **64-65, 73-74**

Firsov, P. B. SR, delegate to 2nd Soviet Congress 1917 from South-Western army. **74**

Gendel'man, Mikhail Yakovlevich, (1881 – 1938). Lawyer. Joined SRs as student in Germany, 1903. In Kiev Soviet 1905. Frequently arrested and imprisoned. In 1917 on Moscow Soviet EC, SR CC and Soviet CEC. Led SR delegates out of 2nd Soviet Congress October 1917. Constituent Assembly deputy, took part in *Komuch* June 1918. Arrested 1920. Tried at SR show-trial, thereafter in prison and exile. Shot. **73, 75, 80**

Gershteyn, Lev Yakovlevich, (1877 – 1935). Worker, revolutionary from 1898, SR. Frequently arrested, imprisoned and exiled, in emigration until 1917. On SR CC from November 1917. Constituent Assembly deputy, took part in *Komuch* June 1918. Among leaders of Irkutsk Political Centre 1920. Arrested by Cheka 1921, tried in SR show-trial 1922, thereafter in prison and exile. **80**

Gizetti, Aleksandr Alekseevich, (1888 – 1938). Writer, journalist, literary critic, sociologist. Noted for studies of Russian writers. Wrote for SR papers 1917. In 1920s worked at Academy of Sciences' library. Arrested and shot 1938. **25**

Gots, Abram Rafailovich, (1882 – 1940). Revolutionary from 1896, SR leader. In SR Fighting Organisation from 1906, imprisoned 8 years from 1907. "Siberian

Zimmerwaldist" in WW1. On Petrograd Soviet EC from March 1917, led SR faction. After October chaired Committee to Save the Motherland and Revolution, advocated armed resistance to Bolsheviks. In 1922 SR trial, death sentence commuted to 5 years. Frequently arrested, died in camp 1940. **19-23, 26-27, 74, 80**

Guchkov, Aleksandr Ivanovich, (1862 – 1936). Major capitalist, among founders of "Union of 17 October", 1905, party chief from 1906. Elected member of State Council, chaired 3ʳᵈ State Duma for a year. Headed Central War Industries Committee from summer 1915. Involved in conspiracies against Nicholas II from autumn 1916. War and Naval Minister in 1st Provisional Government to 30.4.1917. After October – subsidised and backed White armies. Died in France. **28**

Gukovsky, Aleksandr Isaevich, (1865 – 1925). Lawyer, writer, founder-member of SRs. Defencist in WW1, right SR, editor of *Volya naroda*. Mayor of Arkhangel'sk during British intervention, 1918. Emigrated end 1919. Committed suicide. **25**

Gurevich, Vissarion Yakovlevich, (1876 – 1939). Lawyer, narodnik from 1898, worked with Trudovik faction in Duma. In 1917 in Krasnoyarsk Soviet. SR representative on government commission to prepare for Constituent Assembly elections. On Peasant Soviet EC. On SR CC 1917. Constituent Assembly deputy, took part in *Komuch* June 1918. Emigrated 1920, ran Russian historical archive in Prague. **30**

Gus'kov. Petrograd SR, internationalist in 1917. **25**

Hindenburg, Paul Ludwig Hans Anton von Beneckendorff und von, (1847 – 1934). German career soldier, in 1917 Field-Marshal, Chief of General Staff. President of Germany 1925-34. **25, 53**

Hrushevsky, Mikhail Sergeevich, (1866 – 1934). Ukrainian nationalist ideologist and activist; academic historian. Liberal-democratic before 1914, joined Ukrainian SR party 1917. 4.3.1917 elected chairman of Central Rada, Kiev, advocated broad autonomy. After dissolution of Constituent Assembly January 1918, advocated Ukrainian independence. Emigrated 1919, abandoned politics, returned to Ukraine as academic 1924. Elected to USSR Academy of Sciences 1929. **41**

Il'insky, Igor' Vladimirovich (?). Petrograd SR 1917, defencist. **25**

Kamkov (Kats), Boris Davidovich, (1885 – 1938). SR from early 1900s, exiled 1905, escaped abroad 1907. Internationalist in WW1, attended Zimmerwald conference 1915. Returned to Russia April 1917, elected to Petrograd Soviet EC. On Soviet CEC from June 1917. Consistent leftist, supported Soviet power. Among founders of Left SR party. Fell out with Bolsheviks over Brest peace treaty, March 1918. Among organisers of assassination of Mirbach, July 1918. Thereafter underground, in prison or exile. Witness at Bukharin trial, 1938. Shot. **23-26, 29-30, 32, 74**

Kanegisser, Leonid Akimovich, (1896 – 1918). Poet, soldier, People's Socialist. Among Junkers defending Winter Palace from Bolsheviks October 1917. Killed Petrograd Cheka chief Uritsky in revenge for killing of friend. Shot by Cheka. **97**

Kaplan, Fania (Fanni) Efimovna, (Roytblat, Feyga Khaimovna, 1888 – 1918). Anarchist-communist, sentenced to indefinite hard labour 1906 for bombing hotel. In Moscow after February 1917. Attempted assassination of Lenin 30.8.1918. Shot. **97**

Karelin, Vladimir Aleksandrovich, (1891 – 1938). SR from 1907, journalist. Among leaders of large leftist Khar'kov SR organization, 1917, elected chairman of Khar'kov city duma. On Presidium at 2nd All-Russia Soviet congress. Among leaders of Left SR party. In government December 1917 - March 1918. After July 1918 in and out of prison, left politics 1921, but kept contact with other Left SRs. Arrested 1937, witness in Bukharin trial March 1938, shot September. **74, 77-78, 94**

Kerensky, Aleksandr Fedorovich (1881 – 1970). Lawyer, journalist, politician. SR sympathiser in 1905, openly SR member from 1917. Made name as defence lawyer in political trials. Elected to 4th Duma 1912, led Trudovik group. 2.3.1917 joined Provisional Government as Justice Minister. May-September 1917 Army and Naval Minister, Prime Minister from 8.7.1917, C-in-C from 30.8.1917. Overthrown by Bolsheviks, emigrated 1918. **12, 15-16, 28, 31, 35, 52, 57, 60, 64-65, 67**

Kireevsky, Ivan Vasil'evich (1806 – 1856); and Petr Vasil'evich (1808 – 1856). Slavophile writers and ideologists. **61**

Klement'ev. In 1917: Baltic sailor, defencist SR. **24**

Kocherygin, Mitrofan. Tambov peasant, 1917. **44**

Kolchak, Aleksandr Vasil'evich, (1873 – 1920). Tsarist Admiral, former commander of Black Sea Fleet. 18.11.1918 took supreme power in Siberia in coup. Organised White army, controlled all Siberia and Urals early 1919. Pushed back by Reds from May. January 1920 captured near Irkutsk by SRs, shot February. **97-98**

Kolegaev, Andrey Lukich, (1887 – 1937). SR from 1906. Imprisoned, exiled and in emigration before 1917. Headed leftist Kazan' SR organisation from May 1917, held local government and Soviet posts. On Soviet CEC after October, among founders of Left SR party. Agriculture Commissar 25.11.1917 – 24.3.1918. Among founders of Party of Revolutionary Communism, joined Bolsheviks November 1918. Arrested 1936, shot 1937. **74, 98**

Kondrat'ev, Nikolay Dmitrievich, (1892 – 1938). Economist, agronomist, sociologist and political activist. SR 1905-19. Participated in February 1917 events, involved in soviet and government food distribution bodies. Hostile to Bolshevik seizure of power, but worked in Soviet Commissariat of Agriculture after leaving SRs. In 1920s headed Conjuncture Institute and devised economic plans to revive agriculture. Arrested on false charges 1930, shot 1938. **48-50, 98**

Kornilov, Lavr Georgievich, (1870 – 1918). Cossack, career soldier, General. Served in Central Asia and Russo-Japanese war. Commanded frontline infantry divisions from 1914. Captured 1915, famed in Russia after a daring escape 1916. Commanded Petrograd military district March – May 1917. Commander-in-Chief from 19.7.1917. Favoured restoring army discipline through executions etc. Led confused revolt against Provisional Government August 1917, arrested. Escaped November 1917, helped form first White army. Killed in action. **64-65, 67**

Koshelev, Aleksandr Ivanovich, (1806 – 1883). Public figure, editor of Slavophile journals, involved in preparation of peasant reform 1861. **60**

Kovarsky, Il'ya Nikolaevich, (Sventsyansky, Iuda Iotovich, 1880 – 1962). Narodnik from 1899. Doctor. On SR CC from 1907, on right of party. Assistant Mayor of Moscow, 1917. Emigrated 1919 to Paris, from 1940 in New York. **25**

Kraevsky, Andrey Aleksandrovich, (1810 – 1889). Journalist and publisher. Published *Otechestvennye zapiski* from 1839. Progressive to 1848, then monarchist. **61**

Krylenko, Nikolay Vasil'evich, (1885 – 1938). Bolshevik from 1904, student leader 1905-08. Then teacher, in army, in exile etc. until conscripted 1916. Involved in soldiers' committees, arrested after July demonstrations, 1917. After October in military work, conserving army and helping build Red Army. Acted as prosecutor in SR show-trial 1922. USSR Procurator from 1928. From 1936 USSR Commissar of Justice. Arrested and shot. **81, 92**

Kurlov, Pavel Grigor'evich, (1860 – 1923). Tsarist official and police chief. Lt.-Gen. in gendarmes, also held various governorships and Interior Ministry posts. Arrested after March 1917, freed, emigrated 1918. **91**

Lebedev. Petrograd SR in 1917, defencist. **24**

Lenin (Ul'yanov), Vladimir Il'ich, (1870 – 1924). Revolutionary from 1880s, social-democrat. Exiled 1897, emigrated 1900, worked on papers *Iskra* and *Zarya*. Led Bolshevik faction at 2nd RSDRP congress 1903, thereafter unchallenged leader of Bolsheviks. In Russia 1905-07, then in emigration until 1917. Very active as journalist, organiser, theorist and in international socialism. April 1917 returned, set Bolsheviks on uncompromising course, pushed for seizure of power. From October led government, ruled Soviet state until incapacitated by strokes, 1922. **23, 57, 62, 70, 79, 90, 93, 97**

Liebknecht, Karl, (1871 – 1919). German left social-democrat, in SPD from 1900, Reichstag deputy 1912 - 16. First deputy to vote against war credits, December 1914. Imprisoned 1916 for organising anti-war May Day demonstration. Involved with Independent SPD and *Spartakusbund*, one of the founders of the Communist Party of Germany, 1918. Murdered by officers following attempted rising, January 1919. **25**

Lloyd George, David. (1863 – 1945). British Liberal Prime Minister 1916 – 1922. Sabotaged socialist peace efforts in Stockholm 1917. **53**

Lunacharsky, Anatoliy Vasil'evich, (1875 – 1933). Revolutionary from schooldays, social-democrat from 1895. Studied in Zurich under positivist philospher Avenarius. Bolshevik from 1904, in emigration 1906-17. Internationalist in WW1, rejoined Bolsheviks with *mezhrayonka* 1917. In Petrograd City Duma, deputy mayor 1917. Education commissar 1917-29. Prosecution witness at SR show trial 1922. **62**

Luzhenovsky, Gavriil Nikolaevich (1871 – 1906). State official in Tambov *guberniya*, suppressed peasant risings brutally. Assassinated by Mariya Spiridonova on behalf of SRs. **84**

L'vov, Georgiy Evgen'evich, (1861 – 1925). Prince, landowner, zemstvo activist, Tolstoyan. In 1st Duma. Elected Moscow mayor 1913, vetoed by government. Organised Union of Towns and Zemstvos in WW1. Head of Provisional Government March – July 1917. Arrested February 1918, escaped to Omsk, then to USA, raised funds for White cause. **28**

L'vov, Mikhail Ivanovich, (1885 – ?). SR from 1904. In Omsk to 1917, worked in agricultural machine production. Party and peasant soviet worker in Moscow 1917. Arrested several times after 1917, in SR show 1922, thereafter in prison and exile. **73**

Malkin, Boris Fedorovich, (1891 – 1938). SR from 1908, Left SR from 1917, on

PLSR CC. Joined Bolsheviks spring 1918, worked in Soviet press distribution and publishing apparatus to 1938. Arrested and shot. **74**

Marx, Karl Heinrich, (1818 – 1883). German socialist economist, sociologist, historian, philosopher. Author of *Kapital*, ideological inspirer of social-democratic movement. **8-9**

Maslov, Semyon Leont'evich, (1873 – 1938). SR, statistician, economist, writer. In 1917 prominent in co-operative and peasant organisations; Agriculture Minister in 3rd coalition Provisional Government. Abandoned politics after 1917, in leadership of Soviet co-operatives until 1929. Arrested several times after 1930, shot 1938. **35-38**

Mikhaylovsky, Nikolay Konstantinovich, (1842 – 1904). Publicist and ideologist of early narodism, editor of *Otechestvennye zapiski* to 1882, of *Russkoe bogatstvo* from 1892. Convinced opponent of Marxism. **9**

Milyukov, Pavel Nikolaevich, (1859 – 1943). Historian, journalist, public figure, liberal. Imprisoned briefly 1902. Lectured and studied in Bulgaria, UK, France, USA. Founder and leader of Kadet party, editor of its paper, *Rech'*. In 3rd and 4th Dumas, specialised on foreign affairs. Initiated formation of Progressive Bloc 1915. Foreign Minister in 1st Provisional Government, advocated war until victory. Sided with Whites after October 1917, then in emigration in France. **27-30**

Minor, Osip Solomonovich, (1861 – 1934). Son of rabbi, narodnik from 1880s, joined SRs in emigration 1902. Arrested and exiled several times. Right SR in 1917, headed Moscow City Duma. Sharply opposed Bolsheviks, emigrated 1919. **67-69**

Mirbach, Count Wilhelm, (1871 – 1918). German diplomat, ambassador in Moscow April – July 1918. Killed by Left SR Chekists in course of failed rising 6.7.1918. **98**

Mstislavsky (Maslovsky), Sergey Dmitrievich, (1876 – 1943). SR from 1904, army officer in WW1. On EC of Petrograd Soviet and soldiers' section, 1917. Leftist, took part in taking power, October 1917, joined Left SR party. Favoured working with Bolsheviks, opposed LSR rising July 1918. Joined Ukrainian Left SRs 1918, fought in Red Army. After 1921, writer and TU official in Moscow. **73**

Myakotin, Venedikt Aleksandrovich, (1867 – 1937). Writer on *Russkoe bogatstvo*, historian, SR from 1900s, People's Socialist from 1906. Headed Working People's Socialist Party 1917, favoured socialist-liberal coalition. Opposed Bolshevik takeover, founded Union for Regeneration of Russia spring 1918, from summer on White-controlled territory. Imprisoned by Reds 1920, expelled from Russia 1922. **37-39**

Natanson, Mark Andreevich, (1850 – 1919). Revolutionary from early 1870s, narodnik, frequently arrested and exiled. Emigrated to Switzerland 1904. SR from 1905. In charge of party finances. Favoured union of all socialist parties, maintained links with social-democrats. Internationalist in WW1. Returned to Russia May 1917. On EC of Peasant Soviet. Leftist in SR party, joined Left SRs November 1917. On Soviet CEC Presidium after October 1917. Joined Party of Revolutionary Communism September 1918. Left Russia for medical treatment, died in Berne. **11-12, 32, 98**

Nesterov, Ivan Petrovich, (? – 1960). Left SR from Minsk, on Soviet CEC from October 1917. **73**

Nicholas II (Romanov, Nikolay Aleksandrovich), (1868 – 1918). Emperor 1894

– 1917. Abdicated March 1917, shot with family in Urals 17.7.1918. **12, 15, 17, 24, 44-45, 58, 67, 84**

Odoevsky, Vladimir Fedorovich, (1803 – 1869). Prince, writer, philosopher, educator and musicologist. Expressed Slavophile views on the uniqueness of the Russians. **61**

Pereverzev, Pavel Nikolaevich, (1871 – 1944). Lawyer, freemason, Trudovik sympathiser. Noted for brilliant defences in political cases. Imprisoned for protest about Beylis case, 1913. Justice Minister and Procurator 05.05.1917–6.07.1917. Escaped into emigration after October. **31, 57**

Peshekhonov, Aleksey Vasil'evich, (1867 – 1933). Priest's son, writer, economist, statistician. In opposition circles from 1880s, sympathised with narodniks. Wrote for *Russkoe bogatstvo*. SR from 1901. After 1905 favoured creating legal party, broke with SRs 1906, forming People's Socialists. Defencist in WW1. Food Minister 26.5 – 26.8.1917, implemented grain monopoly. Opposed Bolshevik seizure of power, resisted by legal means until autumn 1918, then went south and worked with Whites. In Soviet statistical offices 1921-22, then expelled from Russia. **31**

Petrovsky-Il'enko. Petrograd SR, 1917. **25**

Plekhanov, Georgiy Valentinovich, (1856 – 1918). Founder of Russian Marxism, philosopher, writer. Narodnik from 1876, emigrated 1880, became Marxist. Founded "Emancipation of Labour" group 1883. Neutral in RSDRP split 1903, later closer to Mensheviks. Staunch defencist in war, formed "Edinstvo" social-democratic group, to right of all Menshevik factions. Returned to Russia 1917, defended Provisional Government. Denounced Bolshevism. Already very ill, died in Finland. **8**

Pleve, Vyacheslav Konstantinovich, (1846 – 1904). Tsarist state and police functionary. Head of Police Department from 1881, senator, minister from 1899. Appointed Interior Minister and Chief of Police 1902, encouraged punitive expeditions against peasants and workers and pogroms against Jews. Assassinated by SRs. **10**

Pogodin, Mikhail Petrovich, (1800 – 1875). Historian of Russia, worked at Moscow University, published prolifically. Slavophile until 1860s, later ideologist of Pan-Slavism. **61**

Posse, Vladimir Aleksandrovich, (1864 – 1940). Doctor, lecturer, free-ranging revolutionary. Sympathised with social-democrats in 1900s but did not join RSDRP. Translated and published Marxist classics, propounded mixture of Marxism, anarcho-syndicalism and co-operation. Internationalist in WW1. In 1917 formed own "Union for Property and Labour Equality", supported but did not join Bolsheviks. **62**

Prilezhaev, Ivan Aleksandrovich, (1881 – 1946). Son of village priest, agronomist, SR from 1902. Propagandist, journalist and agitator. Arrested, imprisoned and exiled several times. On SR CC 1917, disenchanted with slow land reform, left party end 1917. Worked in agriculture and food commissariats in Moscow and Ukraine. Joined CP 1931. **80**

Prosh'yan, Prosh Perchevich, (1883 – 1918). SR from 1903. Internationalist in WW1, expelled from SRs in 1917 for participation in July demonstrations. One of the leaders of the Left SRs 1917 - 1918. From 22.12.1917 – People's Commissar of Posts and Telegraphs. Involved in Left SR rising and assassination of German ambassador on 6.7.1918, sentenced in absentia to 3 years. Died 16.12.1918 of typhus. **89-90**

Pumpyansky, Nikolay Petrovich. Siberian SR, on Peasant Soviet CEC 1917, Constituent Assembly deputy 1918, on Soviet CEC 1918. **24**

Raskol'nikov (Il'in), Fedor Fedorovich, (1892 – 1939). From priest's family, Bolshevik from 1910. In navy in WW1. Based at Kronstadt after February 1917. Among organisers of July Days demonstrations in Petrograd, arrested, released October. Held naval and party posts, arrested by British ship during intervention December 1918, held at Brixton prison, exchanged for British officers. Thereafter in army and diplomatic posts. Sacked 1938 while abroad, refused to return to USSR and denounced Stalin. Died in mysterious circumstances. **93**

Rakitnikov, Nikolay Ivanovich, (1864 – 1938). SR organiser and publicist. In *Narodnaya volya* from 1885, arrested, exiled. Founder-member of PSR 1901, on 1st CC, noted for work among peasants. Internationalist in WW1. Deputy Agriculture Minister in Provisional Government. Opposed both Bolshevik takeover and armed struggle against them. Abandoned politics end 1919, worked as statistician and economist. Arrested 1937, shot 1938. **80**

Rakov, Dmitriy Fedorovich, (1881 – 1941). SR from peasant family, schoolteacher. Active in teachers' union 1905-07. On SR CC 1917, elected to Constituent Assembly. In Samara *Komuch* government 1918, arrested by Kolchak. In Prague 1919, sent by SRs to Moscow to organise underground work 1920, arrested. In SR show-trial 1922, thereafter repeatedly imprisoned and exiled. Shot 8.9.1941. **80**

Rivkin, Grigoriy (Girsh) Abramovich, (1877 – 1922). SR-Maximalist. Studied chemistry and electronics at French universities, returned to Russia 1902, joined SRs. Bomb-maker in 1905. Among leaders of Moscow rising December 1905. Arrested and escaped several times, lived abroad 1907-17. From April 1917 worked at Kronstadt port, led SR-Maximalist faction on Kronstadt Soviet. Took part in 2nd and 3rd Soviet congresses. **58-60**

Rudnev, Vadim Viktorovich, (1879 – 1940). Head of Moscow SR organisation from 1905, involved in December 1905 uprising. In exile and prison. Abandoned party work until 1917, worked as doctor. Defencist in WW1. Headed Moscow SRs after February 1917, Mayor of Moscow from July. After October tried organising armed resistance to Bolsheviks. Elected to Constituent Assembly. Supported Denikin's White army and foreign intervention. Emigrated 1919. **11**

Savinkov, Boris Viktorovich, (1879 – 1925). Political activist, journalist, writer, military conspirator. SR 1903-17, in SR Fighting Organization, organized assassinations. 1911-17 in France, served in French army in WW1. 1917 in Russian war ministry, worked with Kerensky, favoured war to victory. Sympathised with Kornilov, expelled from SRs. After October supported Whites, worked with Poles 1920. Returned to USSR 1924, arrested. Died in detention, circumstances unclear. **32**

Sergeev, Nikita. Housepainter in St Petersburg, anarchist before revolution, SR 1917-18, assassinated V. Volodarsky 1918. **97**

Shevyrev, Stepan Petrovich, (1806 – 1864). Russian literary historian and critic, poet, Slavophile. **60**

Shifer, Perets Frimovich. Revolutionary since 1890s, Odessa SR, leftist. In 1919 joined Ukrainian Left SR party. **89**

Shreyder, Aleksandr Abramovich, (1893 – 1930). Lawyer, writer, publisher, SR. Active in Petrograd SRs 1917, on ECs of Petrograd Soviet and Peasant Soviet. Worked closely with Bolsheviks on taking power. Founder of Left SR party. Deputy Justice Commissar winter 1917-18. In semi-legal position after July 1918, emigrated end 1919, published Left SR journals and represented LSR party abroad. Committed suicide. **87-89**

Shteynberg (Steinberg), Isaak-Nakhman Zakharovich, (1888 – 1957). Writer and lawyer, SR theoretician. Joined SRs 1906, exiled 1907, studied law in Germany. In Ufa 1917. Joined Left SRs. People's Commissar of Justice December 1917–March 1918. Arrested several times up to 1923, emigrated. Then in Jewish socialist circles in Germany, Britain and USA. Wrote books on Russian revolution, memoirs etc. **70, 93-94**

Sipyagin, Dmitriy Sergeevich, (1853 – 1902). Tsarist functionary, started in Interior Ministry 1876, held various governorships and other state posts. Interior Minister from 1900. Met growing workers' and peasants' movement with crude repression, assassinated by SRs. **9**

Skobelev, Matvey Ivanovich, (1885 – 1938). Social-democrat from 1903, led strikes in Baku 1905-06. Abroad 1906-12. Elected to 4th Duma, in Menshevik fraction from 1913. Defencist in WW1. Among founders of Petrograd Soviet. On Soviet CEC June-October 1917, Minister of Labour May-September 1917. Tried organising resistance to Bolsheviks October 1917. Left Mensheviks, joined Bolsheviks 1922. Worked in Soviet economic institutions. Arrested and shot 1938. **31**

Sorokin, Pitirim Aleksandrovich, (1889 – 1968). SR from 1905, sociologist, journalist, political functionary. Worked with Trudoviks in Duma, particularly Kerensky. Defencist in WW1, on right of SR party. In 1917 writer on *Volya naroda*, secretary to Kerensky, on Peasant Soviet EC. Elected to Constituent Assembly, imprisoned January-March 1918. Quit politics end 1918, lectured at Petrograd University and institutes. Deported 1922, in USA from 1923, became leading sociologist. **25, 32, 60-63**

Spartacus, (ca 120 BCE – ca 70 BCE). Thracian-born Roman gladiator, escaped slavery and led sustained mass armed slave rebellion against Roman forces. **62**

Spiridonova, Mariya Aleksandrovna, (1884 – 1941). Revolutionary from schooldays, SR, terrorist, imprisoned for life 1906 for assassinating Tambov official Luzhenovsky. Freed by Kerensky March 1917. On far left of SR party, founder of Left SRs. On VTsIK after October. Involved in Left SR assassination of German ambassador Mirbach. Thereafter frequently arrested, exiled, imprisoned on political charges. Sentenced to 25 years 1938, shot 1941. **32, 35-37, 84-85, 93**

Stalin (Dzhugashvili), Iosif Vissarionovich, (1878? 1879? – 1953). Georgian social-democrat from 1898, Bolshevik from 1903. Active in Caucasus RSDRP, and in 1905-07 events. In internal exile 1913-17, March 1917 in Petrograd. Involved in October seizure of power, first nationalities commissar. Held numerous party and state organisational posts, CP General Secretary from 1922. Made this the key party post, became personal dictator of USSR until his death. **99**

Stankevich, Vladimir Benediktovich, (1884 – 1968). People's Socialist (NS), journalist, political functionary. Defencist in WW1, army volunteer. On Petrograd Soviet EC from March 1917. On EC of NS party from June 1917. Close associate of Kerensky, tried to organise armed resistance to Bolsheviks after October. Left NS CC February 1918, lived underground, emigrated to Berlin 1919. Professor in Lithuania to 1944, in USA from 1949. **28**

Stolypin, Petr Arkad'evich, (1862 – 1911). Russian statesman and administrator, from old nobility. Worked in interior ministry from 1889, governor of Grodno 1902, Saratov 1903-06, repressed peasant rebels. 1906-11 Interior Minister and Prime Minister. 1907 dissolved 2nd Duma, fixed electoral law to ensure right-wing dominance. Combined repression with reform, new agrarian law sought to destroy village commune institutions. Assassinated 1911. **11, 46, 98**

Sverdlov, Yakov Mikhaylovich (1885 – 1919). Bolshevik leader, social-democrat from 1901, full-time revolutionary from 1902. Arrested and exiled several times. On Bolshevik CC from 1912. In Petrograd from 1917, headed Soviet CEC after October. Involved in dispersal of Constituent Assembly and drafting Soviet constitution. One of initiators of "Red Terror" in summer 1918. **93**

Teterkin, Ivan Ivanovich, (? – 1918). Worker, SR, active in Petrograd 1917. Candidate CC member 1917-18. Shot by Cheka on party work in Sarapul. **80**

Trotsky (Bronshteyn), Lev Davydovich, (1879 – 1940). Revolutionary from end 1890s, joined RSDRP, 1903-04 Menshevik. Briefly headed 1st Petrograd Soviet 1905, arrested, exiled, escaped to USA. Returned to Russia 1917, joined Bolsheviks with *mezhrayonka*. September 1917 – chairman of Petrograd Soviet. Played key role in October seizure of power. War commissar 1918-24, founder of Red Army. On Politburo 1919-26. Expelled from CPSU 1927, deported 1929, assassinated 1940. **54, 57, 62**

Trutovsky, Vladimir Evgen'evich, (1889 – 1937). Economist and journalist, specialist on local government, SR from 1908. Leading Left SR 1917, after October on Soviet CEC. December 1917 - March 1918 People's Commissar for Local Government Affairs. In hiding after 6.7.1918. Frequently arrested thereafter, as maintained Left SR connections, esp. in Ukraine. Final arrest 1937, shot October. **24**

Tsereteli, Irakliy Georgievich, (1881 – 1959). Georgian and all-Russia politician, social-democrat from 1903, Menshevik. Led social-democratic faction in 2nd Duma 1906 - 07. Exiled to Siberia. In WW1 "Siberian Zimmerwaldist", after February 1917 on EC of Petrograd Soviet. May - July Minister of Posts and Telegraphs, June - October on Presidium of Soviet CEC. Member of Georgian parliament declaring independence 26.5.1918. Emigrated 1921. **31**

Tukhachevsky, Mikhail Ivanovich, (1893 – 1937). Professional soldier, Lt. in WW1. In CPSU and Red Army, successful against Kolchak, Denikin, Kronstadt and Tambov rebellions, failed in Poland. 1920s and 1930s worked on military theory and modernisation of Red Army. Made Marshal of USSR 1937. Tried and shot 1937. **98**

Uritsky, Moysey Solomonovich (1873 – 1918). Social-democrat from mid-1890s, Menshevik from 1903, associate of Trotsky. Internationalist during WW1, in *mezhrayonka* in 1917, joined Bolsheviks. Took part in October rising, became leading figure in Cheka. Assassinated by L. A. Kanegisser. **97**

Ustinov, Aleksey Mikhaylovich, (1879 – 1937). Landowner's son, SR from 1906. In France and Switzerland in WW1, internationalist. Leftist in 1917, favoured peasant land seizures. Active among sailors at Helsinki. Favoured close alliance with Bolsheviks. Expelled from SRs July 1917, and arrested, freed after Kornilov revolt. Founder of Left SR party 1917, founded Party of Revolutionary Communists 1918, merged with Bolsheviks 1920. In Soviet diplomatic service from 1921. **89**

Utgof (Utgof-Deryuzhinsky), Vladimir L'vovich, (1887 – 1937). Son of police chief, SR from 1906. Junior army officer in WW1, army delegate to Petrograd Soviet 1917, headed SR Petrograd military organisation. Constituent Assembly deputy, took part in *Komuch*, Samara, 1918. Then in co-operative work. Arrested 1922, defendant in SR show trial. Thereafter in prison and exile. Shot. **25**

Vedenyapin, Mikhail Aleksandrovich, (1879 – 1938). SR from 1903. Defencist in WW1. Among founders of Irkutsk Soviet 1917. On SR CC from 1917, Chernov supporter. Constituent Assembly deputy, took part in *Komuch*, Samara, 1918. Arrested 1920, defendant in SR show trial. Then in prison and exile, died in camps. **80**

Vol'sky, Vladimir Kazimirovich, (1877 – 1937). Revolutionary from 1897, SR from 1903. Journalist and co-operator. Defeatist in WW1. In Tver' 1917, active in peasant soviets and SR leadership. In *Komuch* 1918. After Kolchak's coup, reconciled to Soviet power. Arrested several times in 1920s and 1930s, shot. **97**

Volodarsky, V. (Gol'dshteyn, Moisey Markovich), (1891 – 1918). Revolutionary from 1905, in Jewish Bund, then Menshevik. Spent time in prison, exile and abroad. Menshevik-Internationalist in WW1, joined Bolsheviks with *mezhrayonka* 1917. After October, press and propaganda commissar, assassinated by SR. **97**

Wilhelm II, (Hohenzollern, Wilhelm), (1859 – 1941). Last Kaiser of Germany, 1888 – 1918. Deposed at end of WW1, fled to Netherlands. **24**

Zatonsky. See **Batrak**.

Zenzinov, Vladimir Mikhaylovich, (1880 – 1953). Merchant's son, educated in W. Europe, where joined SRs. Returned to Russia 1904, in Moscow SR group. On SR CC from 1905. Joined SR Fighting Organization 1906. Exiled 4 years 1910. Defencist in WW1, became close colleague of A. F. Kerensky. Leading SR 1917, involved in *Komuch* and Ufa Directory 1918, emigrated 1919. Active in émigré circles. **32-35, 80**

Zheleznyakov, Anatoliy Grigor'evich, (1895 – 1919). Revolutionary sailor, involved in taking Winter Palace October 1917, head of guard at Tauride Palace, dispersed Constituent Assembly 6.1.1918. Killed in action in civil war. **95-96**

Zinoviev, Grigoriy Evseevich (Radomysl'sky, Evsey Aronovich), (1883 – 1936). S-D from 1901, Bolshevik from 1903. Mainly abroad to 1917, returned to Russia with Lenin. End 1917–end 1925, head of Petrograd/Leningrad Soviet and CPSU. Head of Comintern 1919-26. In blocs with Stalin against Trotsky 1923-25, Trotsky against Stalin 1925-27. Removed from all important positions. Recanted 1927. Arrested end 1934 on (false) charge of complicity in Kirov murder. Main defendant in show trial August 1936, shot. **57, 62**

XVI. Brief chronology of the SRs in 1917

February	27	Petrograd Soviet formed with participation of Kerensky and other SRs.
March	1	Kerensky becomes Justice Minister in Provisional Government.
	2	1st Petrograd conference of SRs.
	3	Moscow conference of SRs.
	4	Central Rada formed in Kiev, chaired by Ukrainian SR M S Hrushevsky.
	15	1st issue of *Delo naroda*, SR paper.
	29	1st All-Russia Conference of Soviets. Dominated by SRs and Mensheviks.
April	3-5	2nd Petrograd conference of SRs.
	8	V M Chernov returns to Petrograd.
	21	Provisional Government decrees establishment of land committees to prepare for agrarian reform.
May	4-28	First All-Russia Congress of Peasants' Soviets, dominated by SRs.
	5	1st coalition government formed, Chernov becomes Agriculture Minister
May June	25- 4	SRs' 3rd party congress, Moscow. Left SRs present separate platforms.
June	3-24	1st All-Russia Congress of Soviets. SRs have 285 out of 822 delegates, Mensheviks 248, Bolsheviks 105.
	25	SRs win 60% of Moscow City Duma vote. SR V V Rudnev becomes mayor.
	29	Chernov presents draft law to transfer land to land committees.
July	3-5	Armed demonstrations in Petrograd. Main SRs denounce them, Left SRs help organise them.
	8	Kerensky becomes Prime Minister. Government promises land reform and greater peace efforts.
	24	Kerensky forms 2nd coalition government.
July August	30- 20	Local government elections. SRs and Mensheviks gain most deputies.
August	12-15	"State Conference" in Moscow of government-picked political notables, chaired by Kerensky.
	25	"Kornilov revolt" begins. All Soviet parties prepare defence of Petrograd.
	26	Chernov resigns from government

27	Kadet ministers resign. Kerensky sacks Kornilov.
30	Kerensky declares himself C-in-C.
September 1	Kerensky declares Russia a republic, forms 5-man Directory to rule country.
14-22	"Democratic Conference" in Petrograd of representatives of Soviets, local authorities, committees etc. SRs largest single party. DC forms "Pre-parliament".
24	Elections to Moscow district dumas. SRs get just just 14% of the votes.
25	Kerensky forms 3rd coalition government.
October 19	Agriculture Minister S L Maslov presents another draft law to transfer land to land committees.
24	Kerensky orders seizure of Bolshevik printing presses. Petrograd Soviet MRC takes counter-measures.
25	Kerensky flees Petrograd. 2nd All-Russia Congress of Soviets opens. Main SRs walk out in protest at seizure of power. Left SRs remain with Bolsheviks.
26	A R Gots heads Committee to Save the Motherland and Revolution.
29	Committee to Save the Motherland and Revolution launches unsuccessful armed revolt of Junkers, Petrograd.
November 11-25	Extraordinary All-Russia Congress of Peasants' Soviets. Dominated by Bolsheviks and Left SRs.
12	Elections to Constituent Assembly
19-28	1st congress of Left Socialist-Revolutionary Party, Petrograd.
November 26- December 5	SRs' 4th party congress. All Left SRs expelled, but party policy moves leftwards.
November 26- December 10	2nd All-Russia Congress of Peasants' Soviets. Dominated by Bolsheviks and Left SRs.

1918

January 5	Constituent Assembly opens. Chernov elected chairman.
6	Constituent Assembly dispersed on Soviet orders.

THE SOCIALIST HISTORY SOCIETY

The Socialist History Society was founded in 1992 and includes many leading Socialist and labour historians, both academic and amateur, in Britain and overseas. The SHS holds regular events, public meetings and one-off conferences, and contributes to current historical debates and controversies. The society produces a range of publications, including the journal *Socialist History*. We can sometimes assist with individual student research.

The SHS is the successor to the Communist Party History Group, established in 1946. The society is now independent of all political parties and groups. We are engaged in and seek to encourage historical studies from a Marxist and broadly-defined left perspective. We are concerned with every aspect of human history from early social formations to the present day and aim for a global reach.

We are particularly interested in the struggles of labour, women, progressive and peace movements throughout the world, as well as the movements and achievements of colonial peoples, black people, and other oppressed communities seeking justice, human dignity and liberation.

Each year we produce two issues of our journal *Socialist History,* one or two historical pamphlets in our *Occasional Papers* series, and members' newsletters. We hold a public lecture and debate in London five times per year. In addition, we organise occasional conferences, book-launch meetings, and joint events with other sympathetic groups.

Join the Socialist History Society!

Members receive all our serial publications for the year at no extra cost and regular mailings about our activities. Members can vote at our AGM and seek election to positions on the committee, and are encouraged to participate in other society activities.

Annual membership fees (renewable every January):

Full UK	£20.00
Concessionary UK	£14.00
Overseas full	£25.00
Overseas concessionary	£19.00

For details of institutional subscriptions, please e-mail the treasurer on francis@socialisthistorysociety.co.uk .

To join the society for 2008, please send your name and address plus a cheque/PO payable to **Socialist History Society** to: SHS, 50 Elmfield Road, Balham, London SW17 8AL.

Visit our websites on www.socialisthistorysociety.co.uk and www.socialist-history-journal.org.uk .